Coping Successfully with Changing Tides and Winds

A Neurosurgeon's Compass

Dr. Jack Kushner

iUniverse, Inc.
New York   Bloomington

Coping Successfully with Changing Tides and Winds
A Neurosurgeon's Compass

iUniverse books may be ordered through booksellers or by contacting:

iUniverse
1663 Liberty Drive
Bloomington, IN 47403
www.iuniverse.com
1-800-Authors (1-800-288-4677)

Because of the dynamic nature of the Internet, any Web addresses or links contained in this book may have changed since publication and may no longer be valid.

ISBN: 978-1-4401-6110-0 (sc)
ISBN: 978-1-4401-6111-7 (dj)
ISBN: 978-1-4401-6112-4 (ebk)

Printed in the United States of America

iUniverse rev. date: 9/1/2009

CONTENTS

INTRODUCTION

Now that the economy is in a downturn, all of us have to think about what we can do to survive. What if this economic downturn becomes a great depression? What if all countries' currencies become worthless? What if the job losses become excessive?

In my first book, *Preparing to Tack: When Physicians Change Careers*, I speak to the issue of what happens when the external environment changes and the situation is beyond your control. This happened to my career and me. I went into medicine intending to practice neurosurgery until the end of my life, but I did not think that the malpractice situation would deteriorate to the point that it has. Nor did I envision the formation of the health maintenance organization (HMO) system in America, which would take so much decision making away from the physician and give it to HMO officials, who are not doctors. But the unthinkable happened, and eventually I enrolled at the University of Maryland in 1987, and began pursuing more education in another field, gaining my master's degree in general administration in the financial track.

Some will lose their jobs as one plant, one corporation, and one small business after the other closes and lets its employees go. This can have a tremendous effect and lead someone to become depressed and feel worthless, as he is no longer able to support himself or his family. Almost everyone wants to work and strives to do something worthwhile. It may be that the best thing a person can do is look at areas not as affected by unemployment. Seek employment in other areas, and if you have to relocate your family, that is what you have to do. Others may have to increase their skills by seeking more education in order to become more employable or more competitive.

It may be necessary to bring all of your assets and resources to bear and be proactive in altering your situation. Certainly no one should go for broke and put all of his or her financial assets in one investment vehicle. Instead, make one boring investment after another in a steady, sustained manner.

CHAPTER ONE:
LINGERIE ON THE FOUNTAIN

When I was born in 1939, the world was an inimical place into which to bring a child. The fingers of war were reaching across the world. The Holocaust was getting into high gear, and anti-Semitism was prevalent everywhere. Almost everyone was concerned about what was happening in Europe. Japan was becoming more aggressive. It was difficult for anyone to make plans.

My mom, Rose Kushner, was born in 1914 in Sheboygan, Wisconsin. Her mother, Golda Feldman, immigrated to the USA around 1890 from Latvia. Her father, Sam Feldman, immigrated to the USA from Lithuania in 1885, ostensibly to avoid being drafted into the tsar's army for twenty-five years.

My father, Louis Kushner, was born in 1908 in Washington DC. His mother was Sarah Kushner, who immigrated to the USA in 1885 from Minsk. His father, Jacob Kushner, immigrated to the USA in 1882 from Kiev. After Sarah and Jacob married, they lived in Washington DC, where my father was born. They lived and worked there until the influenza epidemic in 1918 took its toll with the demise of several of my father's siblings and Jacob, his father. Afterward my father lived with various relatives, worked in a grocery store, and finally moved to Jacksonville, Florida, to be with other relatives. While in Jacksonville, my father worked during the Great Depression delivering bread to grocery stores.

Sam Feldman, my mother's father, was a diminutive man with a harsh, rough voice who worked as a peddler in Wisconsin. He went from village to village with a horse and cart selling dry goods, utensils, some food items, and clothes. This occupation was profitable and served all the rural people well until Sears Roebuck started publishing a catalogue. Sam also served as the town crier and brought news to the people in these small towns. My mom says that their large family (five children) never lacked for anything. She used to say that she never knew anything about the Great Depression until she met my father.

My mother graduated from high school in Manitowoc, Wisconsin, and wanted to attend the University of Wisconsin, but her father, Sam Feldman, did not approve of girls going off to school by themselves. He insisted that she attend college in Oshkosh, Wisconsin, where she could live with relatives. Mom was rebellious, resisted, and went off to Jacksonville, Florida to work at Setzer's grocery store, which was owned by relatives, and she lived with relatives.

So it was at the grocery store in Jacksonville that my parents met. Soon thereafter they were married and moved to Montgomery, Alabama, as other relatives on my father's side were in Montgomery already. And thus I was born in Montgomery, where we lived on Felder Avenue, next door to Scott and Zelda Fitzgerald. My mom would see Zelda at the bank scribbling gibberish on notes while in line. In 1940 Montgomery was still talking about a party the Fitzgeralds gave years earlier, during which most of the invitees threw their lingerie on the fountain on Court Square in downtown Montgomery. The fountain was similar to the one on Piccadilly Circus in London. Montgomery had never seen anything like the Fitzgeralds and their wild lifestyle.

Because of the war and the uncertainty created by the military draft, Dad started a small grocery store on Grove Street. My parents initially rented a house on Felder Avenue but later bought a house at 914 National Street in Ridgecrest. Since my dad was not drafted until the end of the war, in 1945, he started a larger grocery store at the corner of Oak and Mill Streets, where he worked for the remainder of his working life. In the meantime, my brother Sheldon was born in 1942, and Harold was born in 1947. Every Friday my parents put ten dollars in a drawer to save for college. With that money they were able to educate two doctors and one lawyer.

I started kindergarten on Fairview Avenue across from Huntingdon College. Mrs. Ingalls, a parent of another child, took me to school every day. She had three children standing up in the backseat, three sitting down in the backseat, and three more standing up on the floor of the backseat. All nine of us were students at the same kindergarten. I also started kindergarten at Temple Beth Or on Sundays. That was when I had the first indication that I was color-blind to red and green, as are one out of twelve men. A girl in my class seemed to be upset that I colored a horse purple and called me an idiot.

After World War II, many parents felt the best education for their children was in a military school. In Montgomery there were two such schools, Starke University School and Hurt School. Because there was a large military population in Montgomery at Maxwell Air Force Base and Gunter Air Force Base, plenty of students were attending these schools. And so it was that I left the kindergarten years and enrolled in Starke School at the age of five.

Mrs. Fant was my teacher and would be my teacher in the second and fifth grades as well. There were only five of us in the first grade. Although some students boarded at the school, I continued to live at home with my family. This was truly an example of *Necessary Losses* as described in the book by Judith Viorst, as that separation from my parents was necessary but painful.

Our first grade class was in the same room as the second grade class, which enabled us to pick up pearls from their instructions as well as our own. One day I asked Mrs. Fant the identity of the person in the picture on the wall. She looked at me and said that she was flabbergasted that I did not know who it was. I thought perhaps it was George Washington, but then she humiliated me by asking others in both classes if they knew. Someone in the second grade blurted out that the picture was of President Roosevelt. I was so embarrassed that I started crying, and Mrs. Fant sat me on her lap to calm me down.

Even at this young age we marched and marched. We even marched in the parade down Montgomery Street to celebrate Armistice Day on November eleventh. Spectators pointed to our class, stating that we made cute soldiers.

Toward the end of the first year at Starke, plans were made for the commencement exercises. One of the events was a mandatory school dance, which every cadet was required to attend with a date. I had noticed Rose Mohr at Sunday school and thought she would be the right date. The only problem was that I did not have the nerve to ask her, so Mom rehearsed with me just what I should say. One day I called her and asked her to go to the dance with me, at which time she started crying and gave the phone to her mother. Then I started crying and gave the phone to my mother. The mothers decided that at age six I did not need a date. So I attended the dance with Mom. I didn't speak to Rose for ten years, as I was so humiliated and embarrassed because she told other members in the class that I had asked her to the dance.

Two years later, when I was in the third grade, my brother Sheldon (age five) was in the first grade. The Civil War was still in the memory of those who were grandparents, and people still spoke about it as if it were yesterday. The first grade teacher asked my brother, "Sheldon, aren't both of your parents Yankees?"

Sheldon was so embarrassed that he responded, "Yes, they are, but they have lived so long with us that they act like the rest of us."

Sundays were the loneliest days, as all of our Christian friends went to different places of worship. Because I attended a military school and a Jewish temple, I was getting the feeling that I was different from the other kids. This was especially so on Jewish holidays and Christian holidays, as there were not many Jewish families in Montgomery. I did not experience any anti-Semitism at this age, but peer acceptance was important.

Our neighborhood was an exceptional one in that we had so many playmates. There were at least fifteen boys and four girls in the neighborhood, which enabled us to play all sorts of games and sports. All of the parents raised all of the kids, as we went to the various houses from time to time. This was such an innocent time—we were safe from fears such as kidnapping or other criminal activity.

Unfortunately, we all went barefoot and did not have any immunizations. One day while we were playing hide-and-seek, Hilton Starr stepped on a dog bone. I can still see the image of his father, Sergeant B. Starr, who had just returned from the war in the Pacific, holding Hilton's foot in a bucket of water under the weeping willow tree. Hilton was taken to the hospital at Maxwell Air Force Base, where he died ten days later from lockjaw or tetanus.

About two weeks later Joe Van Wezel brought Bart Starr in his arms back to his house. Bart had been standing on the seat of his bicycle, fell, and hit his head on the pavement. Bart had a concussion and recovered. These two episodes piqued my interest in the mysteries of medicine, and I never forgot them. I personally witnessed these two events and was intrigued by the treatment of injury and disease.

Our neighborhood was a mini training camp for football. In the evenings Bart Starr had several of us running along the shadow of a telephone pole, while someone else would tackle him. This served as a boundary for our tackling practice. We never did any particular exercises to develop our muscles, but we practiced passing the ball, tackling, blocking, and pass defense with Bart as our mentor. Bart stressed that we should place our head in the opponent's soft abdomen so as to not take any of the punishment. He also scheduled National Street to play football against Ridgecrest Street. From that competition, many went on to play Little League football. I played for Capital Chevrolet but was never as good an athlete as Sheldon, who went on to play for Sidney Lanier High School and was selected as an all-city player.

Because we all played together and because our parents looked after all of the kids as if they were their own, we really had a marvelous neighborhood. Sergeant B. Starr always told me that our neighborhood was exceptional. Not only did we live in a wonderful neighborhood, but my parents sent my brother and me to various camps during the summer. Initially we went to Camp Grist in Selma, Alabama, for ten days for swimming, archery, crafts, and various sports. Later we also went to Camp Rotary outside of Wetumpka, where I eventually became a counselor. The most demanding camp was Camp Tukabatchee, a Boy Scout camp, outside of Pratville, Alabama, where we worked on our various merit badges. We had rigorous training in swimming, lifesaving, and other aquatic activities. That is where I made the most progress toward obtaining the Eagle Scout award and was inducted into the Order of the Arrow, an honor camper organization.

All of us felt very secure growing up in this protected environment and neighborhood. This experience always served as wonderful reference point as we grew up and realized the insecurity and uncertainty of the world around us.

CHAPTER TWO:
TWO WORLDS, SEPARATE AND
UNEQUAL

The Korean War continued and Eisenhower ran for the presidency on the pledge that he would end the war, which he did. The number of parents who wanted to send their kids to a military school diminished, so Starke University School ceased to exist, and I transferred to Baldwin Junior High School. Mr. Watts, the principal, told my mom that my outstanding grades would drop a little since the school could not give me the personal attention that the private military school did. But my grades were still high despite what he said. I loved school and was challenged to continue learning and obtaining an education.

In addition to the schoolwork, I was active in the Boy Scouts. Troop 101 met every Monday evening at St. James Methodist Church, which my mom—even though she was Jewish and brought her sons up Jewish—helped found with Mrs. F. Ingram, Mrs. B. Starr, and Mrs. W. Thomas. While in the Boy Scouts I earned the Eagle rank when I was thirteen and was the first Boy Scout in Alabama to earn the Ner Talmud Award for demonstrating significant knowledge of the Jewish religion. In addition, I won the Good Citizenship Award given by the Daughters of the American Revolution. This award was for participating in community activities such as decorating the military cemetery on Memorial Day, planting trees, cleaning up the city, and helping to build small bridges in the city park.

In the afternoons and on the weekends, I worked with Rabbi Atlas on my Bar Mitzvah. A few years ago I felt fortunate to call Rabbi Atlas, who was in his nineties and living in Miami, to tell him that I have been to many Bar Mitzvahs since mine, but I have never seen such a beautiful Bar Mitzvah as the one he put on for me. He worked with me so that I could conduct the entire Friday night and Saturday morning service in Hebrew, read from the Torah, and deliver a speech that my dad helped me write. I was extremely proud to have a Bar Mitzvah and was proactive in seeking out this education.

During those years I became much more aware of racial discrimination in Alabama. I saw that the black kids went to dilapidated schools and had an inferior education. The black adults did only menial tasks, such as yard work, or they worked for the Caucasians as domestic helpers. Only black men collected the trash. The black population was completely separated and segregated and could not eat in white restaurants, drink from white water fountains, use white bathrooms, swim in white pools, or visit white parks and libraries.

In history class, the idea hit me that just a few more years would mark the hundredth anniversary of the Civil War and still the blacks were treated as second-class citizens. The blacks were considered by definition not creditworthy, and hence they could not obtain credit for a mortgage to buy a house. Jim Crow laws were in effect, so the black students attended inferior schools, sat in the back of the bus, attended separate churches, and had separate sports. Their lives were completely separate from the lives of the white people, and socially there was no contact.

For that matter, no Jews were allowed at the Montgomery Country Club, and the social lives of Christians and Jews were separate for the most part, except in our neighborhood. As a Jewish family, we could not belong to the Montgomery Country Club and hence could not learn how to play tennis and golf. These activities were only available in private clubs at that time.

CHAPTER THREE:
NOT AS A STRANGER

In 1954 I enrolled at Sidney Lanier High School, which had about 1,300 students. This was the only white high school in Montgomery, although they were building Lee High School, another school for white students on the other side of the city. Sidney Lanier High School had a strong academic program, and I had excellent teachers.

Ms. Kate Clarke taught all of us Latin, and many stayed with her for five years including the Latin taught in junior high school. She got so passionate and theatrical teaching us that one day she looked out the window and saw Caesar's troops coming across the parking lot. She ran to the other side to see Vercingetorix coming to attack, and while she was strutting across the room, the elastic in her underpants snapped and slid to her ankles. There was total silence in the room as she slowly stepped out of her underpants, put them in a drawer and continued teaching. After class ended, word about the event spread all over the school.

We also had excellent teachers in French, History, Algebra, Geometry, and English, and our students won a large number of scholarships to prestigious colleges and universities. Two boys went on to West Point, one to the Air Force Academy, and one to the U.S. Naval Academy in Annapolis.

There were so many extracurricular activities at Lanier. I belonged to the Latin Club; French Club; Thespian Society; Radio Club; Public Speaking, or Toastmasters Club; and the Hi-Y, which took the place of high school fraternities. The thinking was always that these activities helped with college acceptance, which probably was not true. All of these activities served to keep the students busy and, for the most part, out of trouble. In addition, we had a school play in the spring. I had the part of Wayne Frake in *State Fair* my senior year.

I did make an effort to go out for football at Lanier, weighing only 110 pounds. I went to spring practice, which lasted a few weeks. One day toward the end of the session, I told the coach that I had to go to the dentist the next day. He put his arm around my shoulder and said, "Son, don't worry about a thing. Go ahead to the dentist and take care." A few days later the blue team players were listed on the bulletin board with their substitutes, and the white team was listed along with their substitutes. I was not listed at all and got the message that I really did not have a future with high school football at Lanier High School.

The civil rights struggle continued unabated during those years. On my sixteenth birthday in 1955, I went with my father to see a movie, *Not as a Stranger*, starring Frank Sinatra. This movie was about medical students going to medical school and internship, and I was interested, as I already knew that I wanted to go into medicine. I am not sure exactly when I decided I was going to enter medicine, but I idolized our family doctor and was impressed by the only neurosurgeon in Montgomery.

As we came out of the Empire Theater that day, a Montgomery city bus going to Cleveland Avenue was stopped and there were lots of policemen. We inquired as to what was happening and were told that there was a crazy Negro woman, Rosa Parks, who thought she should not give up her seat for a white man and move to the back of the bus. She was hauled off, fingerprinted, and put in jail for violating the Jim Crow laws of segregation. Shortly afterward, our maid could no longer take the bus to work as the bus boycott started and lasted a few years. The black citizens, with Dr. Martin Luther King as their leader, had their own system of transportation, which the white policemen harassed, and many blacks walked to work.

My thoughts on this at that time were that I knew that segregation was wrong and what the white policemen were doing was wrong. But who was I at age sixteen to challenge the laws of the state of Alabama? In fact, one could not speak out on this travesty due to fear for the safety of one's family. The prevailing sentiment in the city was that segregation was the way things were and should be. After all, that was the way things had been for years and years, and no outside agitators from the North were welcomed. When Northern rabbis and Jewish activists came to Montgomery on Freedom Rides, they made their points, but they also made life difficult for the Jewish citizens in the South who lived there with their non-Jewish neighbors, who would still be there after the Northern activists returned to their homes.

Despite the civil rights excitement in my area, my life went on fairly normally as I pursued my studies and applied to various colleges. I knew that my father's grocery store was small and that his income was limited, and I was conscious of the cost of going to any university. I applied to Tulane, Duke, Alabama, and Washington and Lee. Although I was accepted to all of them, Tulane gave me a scholarship, which sealed the deal. My mom and I went to New Orleans on the train for the initial interview and then to help me move into the dormitory and get settled. I went with jeans, black loafers, and a few items packed in one suitcase, nothing like the amount of possessions taken by my daughters to college years later. I was excited about going to Tulane University, and I was nervous about competing with students from all over the world. It seemed that everyone was pre-med and wanted to be a doctor.

CHAPTER FOUR:
YEARS OF WONDER

Going off to Tulane University was one of the most exciting ventures in my life. I was assigned to Irby House. My first roommate was Kraig Klossom, who was from Montgomery and had attended Lanier High School with me. Later I would room with Lenny Hoffman from Houston and with Ken Heller from Denver.

I took all sorts of examinations so that Tulane could place me in the appropriate classes. I quickly learned that although I placed in junior year Latin, I was not sufficiently prepared for chemistry and calculus classes and was not placed in the advanced classes. Besides the academic challenges, the social scene also competed for my time and attention. One competing force was what was called Pledge Week, during which the various fraternities courted the freshmen. This was the first time in my life that anti-Semitism hit me in the face.

Although I was disappointed by the discrimination, I was neither angry nor ashamed. As a matter of fact, I had a sense of pride that I was invited to be in a fraternity and had never had so much contact with other young Jewish men who were exceptional in many ways. There were four Jewish fraternities, which had been started because the other fraternities did not accept Jewish students. Zeta Beta Tau (ZBT) and Sigma Alpha Mu (SAM) courted me aggressively, and I decide to accept ZBT. I felt that one of the activities of the fraternities was blatant anti-Semitism: when SAM played ZBT in football, which was called the "Nose Bowl."

I have always felt guilty about joining a fraternity because my parents really could not afford to pay fraternity bills for lavish entertainment. Since neither of my parents had a college education, they did not know that the information we had, that medical schools looked to determine whether the applicant was well rounded and accepted by his peers, was inaccurate. This misinformation was learned from other students who had been accepted to medical school. I later learned that fraternity membership had no bearing on medical school acceptance.

I was always worried about the quota system that was in effect for Jewish students trying to gain admission to medical schools. My father used to tell me that the authorities in Alabama were actually saving a place for me at the University of Alabama. His thinking was that less than 1 percent of the population in Alabama was Jewish, and since the quota limited Jewish students to 5 percent, they were therefore saving a place for me. Unfortunately, my dad did not take into consideration that almost all of the Jewish parents were telling their children the same thing, so there was plenty of competition for medical school.

For the two years at Tulane, I worked five hours a week in the admission office stuffing envelopes with Tulane bulletins, which were sent all over the world. This work was for my scholarship to Tulane. This was important because during the middle of the second year at Tulane, I was approached and asked to participate in a new program in which I would go to England for a year of study. The University of Sheffield was chosen by the Tulane administration, and this experience would be extended to others later as the Junior Year Abroad. Furthermore, I would not have to work for my scholarship since I would be in England, yet Tulane would pay for my tuition.

At that time transatlantic travel was mostly by ship. That was my first time on a ship, and it was a lot of fun. The trip on the *Liberte* was enhanced because there were Fulbright scholars as well as an Oxford scholar on the ship. We were introduced to European cuisine and to the experience of hearing other languages, such as French and Italian. About eighteen students from Tulane and Newcomb College were going abroad, with Dr. Joseph and Gloria Cohen as our advisors and *locus parentis*.

When I arrived at the University of Sheffield after a sightseeing tour of England by bus, I was assigned to Crewe Hall. This was a huge dormitory with individual rooms and a large, well-trimmed yard and tennis courts. All students wore black gowns for dinner. Students were there from all over the world, including Kenya, South Africa, India, and Pakistan, and there were two from Hungary who had escaped on foot after the rebellion in 1956.

The Sheffield academic office did not understand that I wanted to take courses in the Faculty of Arts and the Faculty of Science as well as the medical school, as their students only stayed in one faculty. But they allowed me to take Modern British History, Ancient Roman History, Modern European History, Philosophy, Organic Chemistry, and Physical Chemistry.

I befriended several guys, two of whom have remained my friends to this day. I was immediately asked to give two speeches at the Student Union. The reason I was asked was because I was the very first American student at the University of Sheffield. The others were fascinated with America and wanted to learn more about our country. The first speech was to explain in detail the segregation policy of the Southern states. This was difficult to do in view of the fact that so many of the Sheffield students were of different races, and they all knew about the racist policies in the USA. This was one of the most difficult tasks I have ever had. I wanted to defend my country and was having difficulty doing that. My best defense was to say that integration would just take time and everyone would have to have patience. But most of the other students did not buy that explanation. They retorted that one hundred years had passed since our Civil War and that was more than enough time.

For my second speech, I was asked to compare college experiences in the USA to the universities in England, but I really did not know much about the British system when I first arrived at Sheffield. All of the students at Sheffield were on government grants, which were renewable depending on their grades. Hardly any of the students had cars, but the few who did were from other countries. I found myself trying to defend American college life. What were fraternities? How does one get accepted? What is a pledge? What are all those lavish parties about? How is it determined that someone is neat or cool and fraternity material? What about those who are not accepted into any fraternity? Where do the fraternities get all that money for these parties? How does fraternity life fit in with the pursuit of a college education? The speech was accepted and well received by the British students, but they did not approve of our wasteful lifestyle and our conspicuous consumption.

Years later I learned from the students that one of the things that stood out about me was an unusual sound emanating from my room. None of the students had a typewriter then, and I did. I typed all of my letters and notes. They listened to my clickety-clack as it permeated the dormitory. Even though I stood out with my American typewriter and my American clothes, every night after dinner I was invited to join the other students in the common room, where someone played the piano and others had a beer and played darts. We then retired to our rooms to study, and someone would come to my room to announce that the pub would close in thirty minutes, so we had to run to the pub. I thought this habit was strange then and still do, as I did not drink alcoholic beverages to the extent that I couldn't wait until the next day to have a beer. But that was the way the students behaved.

While there we would drink warm beer and discuss politics. Then we would stop by the fish and chips shop, get fish with vinegar on a newspaper, and eat it while we returned to someone's room. There we would drink coffee, eat toast, and continue to debate politics. It was an unusual way to spend one's time, and I would surmise that I would study more the next night, but the next night would be the same scenario. I used to think at the time that this was a distraction from my education, but now that I look back, I think that this was an important and integral part of my education, even though I did not have an exam on these discussions.

I made some lifelong friends while at Sheffield. Although Dave Rewhorn passed away last year, I enjoyed visiting him in England, and both he and his wife visited us in the USA. My last visit with him and Brenda included a visit to the plague village at Eym just outside of Sheffield. (This is the village that my niece by marriage, Geraldine Brooks, described in her novel, *Year of Wonder*.) I have also maintained my friendship through the years with Lewis Dann, who really guided me through the initial weeks at the university, and particularly Organic Chemistry, which he had already had prior to entering the University of Sheffield. Lewis and Nancy have visited us in the USA, and we have visited them several times while in England. Lewis retired recently as an anesthesiologist, and Nancy has retired as a radiologist. Lewis and I were avid sailors during our earlier years.

To prepare for the year abroad, I had gone to summer school one summer at Huntingdon College in Montgomery, Alabama, for a few courses. I also went to summer school at Tulane one summer to take additional courses. While at Tulane I was elected to Alpha Epsilon Delta, a premedical honor society, and to Eta Sigma Phi, a Latin honorary society. Although membership in these organizations did not give me any extra credits toward my bachelor's degree, they indicated that my grades were more than adequate, which enabled me to graduate ahead of time. So at the end of my year at Sheffield, I had enough credits to receive a bachelor's degree in history from Tulane University and did not have to return to Tulane for a fourth year. Because of this situation, Tulane changed the rules, and now all students must return to Tulane for their fourth year, regardless of the number of credits they have. Tulane took this position because they felt that students should spend a certain amount of time at the university that grants them a degree.

In 1960 I entered medical school at the University of Alabama in Birmingham. I had been accepted at Tulane University Medical School, but I did not apply for a scholarship, and they did not offer me one. I knew that my father still had two more children to put through college. I never regretted going to the University of Alabama School of Medicine as far as the education was concerned, because the school had everything one could ask for and then some. In fact, it was the best-kept secret in the country, as it was and is one of the best medical centers in America. The educational experience was rigorous, and we could hardly do anything else but study, study, and study. The University of Alabama School of Medicine is the largest employer in Birmingham and has grown exponentially.

CHAPTER FIVE:
LETTERS FROM ANNETTA

Besides the medical education, three other events during those years stand out in my mind: the civil rights struggle in Birmingham, the Tropical Medicine Fellowship to Panama, and the assassination of President John F. Kennedy. While I was studying at the medical school in Birmingham and spending every day in the laboratory, preparing for almost daily exams, the civil rights issue was gaining momentum throughout the country, especially in Birmingham. Martin Luther King led demonstrations and was jailed in 1963, after which he wrote "Letter from a Birmingham Jail." There were lunch counter demonstrations, and Governor Wallace stood in the doorway in Tuscaloosa at the University of Alabama to prevent black students from entering the university. The mayor was attacking black demonstrators with billy clubs, water hoses, and ferocious dogs.

I think the worst part was the bombing of a black church one Sunday morning, which killed four little girls. I was called to the ER to care for them as I was rotating on the surgical service. All four little girls were dressed in their Sunday best, but all were dead. I felt nauseated and ashamed as I looked at those girls. I was to learn later that these girls were good friends with Secretary of State Condoleezza Rice.

Toward the end of my junior year in medical school, I was offered the opportunity to study tropical medicine in Panama. Louisiana State

Medical School sponsored this program. Some students went to Central American countries and saw patients with various diseases peculiar to that area. I worked with Dr. Sunthorn Sirhonge at the Gorgas Medical Laboratory in Panama City, Panama, which was separate from the Gorgas Hospital in the Canal Zone. We went out in the rural area in Darien, collected serum from birds, and returned to the Gorgas Laboratories, where we ran complement fixation tests and hemoglobin agglutination (HA) and hemoglobin inhibition (HI) tests to determine which viruses were in the area.

At other times I made rounds with Dr. Fletcher at the Santo Tomas Hospital. The writing was on the wall, as there literally was a lot of graffiti on the walls claiming that Panama deserved to own the Panama Canal and that the United States should turn it over to Panama. Even then there were tensions between the citizens of Panama and Americans. Years later the United States gifted the Panama Canal to the country of Panama.

I learned a lot, but I did wonder what my experience would have been otherwise, as initially I was supposed to go to Rhodesia, now Zimbabwe. I was going to work in a hospital there, but I received a letter stating that they did not think a Jewish medical student would fit in with the Christian missionary hospital. At the time I was disappointed and irritated, but as things turned out Panama was an excellent choice.

Prior to going to Panama I went on a tour of possible places for my internship. I took a train to Washington and had an interview at George Washington University Hospital. While in Washington, I had a blind date with Annetta Horwitz, which was arranged by my cousin, Dr. David Kushner, who had actually delivered her about twenty years previously. Annetta was a student at Vassar College in Poughkeepsie, New York. I corresponded with her while I was in Panama . We were attracted to one another from the start, and our correspondence was the glue that kept us together while we were separated. Annetta wanted me to take her to the jungle one day as a Peace Corps participant, but neither of us were ever in the Peace Corps..

Upon my return from Panama, I spoke with her on the phone often and corresponded with her frequently. During Christmas vacation of 1963, we became engaged, and we were married in Washington DC on June 21, 1964, after no more than six dates. We have had a good marriage, even though I tell people that we have been fighting harmoniously for forty-five years. I still have not put the wedding pictures in an album—waiting to see if this marriage is going to take.

During my last year at the University of Alabama School of Medicine, I was rotating on the obstetrics and gynecology service. One day as we finished delivering a baby, someone told us that the president had been shot. Everyone stopped what he or she was doing and became glued to the television. Dan Rather was reporting all day from Dallas. Everyone was affected by the tragedy. The entire medical center seemed to stand still in sadness.

Before the school year ended, I was to assist a gynecologist with surgery as a second assistant. The surgeon had a reputation as being gruff, without a personality, and he suffered fools poorly as well as medical students. As the operation started, he started complaining about everything I did and kept saying, "Goldstein, hold that retractor," "Goldstein, stand here," "Goldstein, hold that instrument," et cetera. I think he knew that Goldstein and I had something in common, and I was not to disabuse him of that idea.

After taking the National Board Medical Exams and the Alabama State Board exams, I headed to Washington to get married and start an internship at George Washington University Hospital. We were married June 21, 1964, at the Willard Hotel in Washington DC. This is a historic hotel, where Abe Lincoln stayed and met with various people during his presidency. Annetta's parents gave us a huge, magnificent wedding. Unfortunately our marriage got off to a shaky start, as our parents disagreed about the invitation list. But somehow we survived, and our parents began to speak to each other again years later.

CHAPTER SIX:
STREET WITHOUT JOY

I started my surgical internship at George Washington University Hospital on July 1, 1964. My duties consisted of examining all the patients admitted to the hospital on the floor to which I was assigned, arranging for all their tests and examinations, and following them through surgery. This consisted of obtaining histories of their medical conditions and performing physical exams. Then I wrote the necessary pre-op orders, did an EKG, drew blood for the various tests, and reviewed with the patients the surgery that would be done the next day. We spent innumerable hours in the operating room (OR) assisting on almost every kind of surgical procedure throughout the year.

One of the attending surgeons was my father-in-law, Dr. Alex Horwitz, who was the first Jewish surgeon trained at the Mayo Clinic. Dr. Horwitz taught the interns one hour a week, and he assigned everyone a topic. The topic about which I was to speak to the other interns and residents was the various hernias that we could repair. I wrote out my speech and practiced with my new wife, Annetta, who saw it as her mission to work on toning down my Southern accent. One of the hernias to be discussed was an umbilical hernia. This could have two different pronunciations, and Annetta had me practice her version. One could accent the "bil" or accent the "ica." When the day came for me to give my talk and I came to this word, only "umb, umb, umb," would come out, until finally I said it the Alabama way.

The year went very fast, as I was on duty thirty-six hours and off twelve hours. I was so busy that I didn't have time to think about the time element. I went home every other night. Annetta would come to the hospital every other evening and join me for dinner in the hospital cafeteria. She was working for the *National Geographic* magazine in customer relations and took care of our pet hamster, Champ Lyons, named after the chief of surgery at the University of Alabama.

Toward the end of the year, I rotated in the emergency room and worked for twenty-four hours on and twenty-four hours off. I served as the only doctor in the emergency room and saw anywhere from sixty to eighty patients in a twenty-four-hour period. One Sunday night during the last week of June 1965, during the height of the civil rights struggle, I saw a black female who complained of indigestion. I checked her blood pressure and it read 60/40, and then all of a sudden she had a cardiac arrest. I put her supine on the examining table and started cardiopulmonary resuscitation. I called for help and a Code Blue was in effect. Numerous residents and anesthesia personnel came through the waiting room immediately. We all tried everything to resuscitate her, but we failed to save her. After almost everyone left, a big black fellow walked into the ER and inquired about his mother. The nurse told him that his mother had died.

He said, "How can that be? My mom just had indigestion; I dropped her off and went to obtain a parking space. Where is the doctor?" The nurse pointed toward me.

He then said, "If my mom had been white, she would have had an older doctor. Because my mom was black, they gave her this boy doctor. I am going to kill that doctor right now." The police grabbed him, restrained him, and put handcuffs on him. They took him through the waiting room to jail.

I gathered my thoughts, as I was visibly shaken by the threats, and picked up another chart and said "next."

My next patient stood up and said, "I saw what happened to that lady with indigestion. I have a chicken bone caught in my throat. I think I will wait until tomorrow to return and hope an older doctor is on duty."

I was on duty in Washington for just a few more days, and every time I said "next," I was worried that the angry son would be there with a weapon. But I left for Ann Arbor, Michigan, the last day of June 1965, where I would start my surgical residency.

Annetta and I drove from Washington DC to our new apartment on Island Drive Court in Ann Arbor. Our furniture was to arrive one week later, so we camped out as best as we could. The University of Michigan was huge and had a large residency program—350 residents, in fact. I had already been accepted by Dr. Eben Alexander at Wake Forest Medical Center in Winston-Salem, North Carolina, to start a neurosurgery residency in 1968, so I would be doing a surgical residency in Ann Arbor and would spend as much time as I could with the neurosurgical program. I attended the neurosurgical conferences and really enjoyed listening to Dr. Edgar Kahn, professor of neurosurgery and chairman of the Department of Neurosurgery; Dr. Richard Schneider; and Dr. Elizabeth Crosby, a neuroanatomy expert who spent some of her time at the University of Alabama in addition to the University of Michigan.

In addition to the surgical rotations through general surgery, urology, orthopedics, and gynecology, during which I served as an assistant, I did witness a number of neurosurgical operations. It seemed to me that because there were so many residents in the surgical programs, they did not get much experience in the OR operating independently until after they completed their residencies and returned as fellows in surgery. Neurosurgery already requires six to eight years of residency training, and this arrangement prolongs the training experience. As surgical residents, we spent a great deal of time discussing the various diseases and surgical conditions.

In any case, I witnessed many surgical procedures, attended numerous surgical conferences, did a lot of studying, and continued to progress in the surgical world. As almost everyone knew that I would be taking a neurosurgical residency at Wake Forest Medical Center, we never felt that we were really accepted at the University of Michigan. Annetta spent her time at the Horace Rackham Graduate School working on her master's degree in English. We were expecting our first child in February 1966. The Vietnam War was heating up, and more and more of my friends were going to Vietnam.

I was enrolled in the Berry Plan, which meant that after my first year of residency I would go into the military for two years. I felt very strongly that we as a country should be in Vietnam and believed my government when the leaders said it was a necessary war that we had to win. I had been to Panama and had studied tropical medicine and had had two years of surgical training experience.

My orders came and said that I was to be in the U.S. Army as a 3150 D doctor, which is a partially trained general surgeon. I was to be assigned to a post in Virginia for six months, then to Greenland for six months, back to Virginia, and then back to Greenland. In Greenland I would be without any family. This was a crisis as far as I was concerned. I felt that I wanted to be in Vietnam, that I was trained to go to Vietnam, and I wanted to be a part of the war effort. I felt that I would be a craven on the battle's edge stationed in Greenland, and I did not like that image. I also knew that Annetta, with a new baby girl, would not want me to go to Vietnam. I felt that if I did go and was injured in any way, Annetta should not be part of the decision.

So it was with a heavy heart that I flew to Washington in March 1966 and talked with people at the Pentagon and the Navy building. They said that since I had a child and already had my orders, I should just go ahead and plan to go to Virginia and to Greenland. Upon my return to Ann Arbor, without discussing it with Annetta, I wrote to the place that issued my orders, to the president, and to the Pentagon, volunteering to go to Vietnam.

A great deal of thought went into the decision. While I was an intern at George Washington University Hospital, one of my patients was Bernard Fall. He was in the hospital on the urology service because he had what was called retroperitoneal fibrosis, ostensibly caused by a drug. He referred me to some of his books, which I read, namely *Street Without Joy*, *Viet-Nam Witness*, and *The Two Viet-Nams*. We used to discuss American involvement, and he cautioned against getting involved. He predicted that we could never win such a war. A few years later, after he recovered, he returned to Vietnam and was killed when he stepped on a mine.

When many people think about Vietnam now, the very word conjures up images of five photos that were spread all over the world. One picture was taken when a Buddhist monk set himself on fire to protest the policies of the Ngo Dinh Diem regime, which the United States supported. A second photo was of Kim Phuc running down Highway 1 fleeing a napalm attack by South Vietnamese airplanes. A third photo was of Nguyen Ngoc Loan shooting a Vietcong in the head. The fourth photo was of the My Lai Massacre, when American combat troops murdered many civilians. The fifth and final photo that circled the world was of a helicopter leaving Saigon evacuating people.

The entire collection is shown in *Lies My Teacher Told Me* by James W. Loewen.

I have a collection of photos that show American soldiers treating Vietnamese civilians in a program called Medcap. I also have photos of Americans operating on Vietnamese trying to save lives. I did not see any atrocities by Americans against Vietnamese civilians.

A few weeks after I wrote the letters, Annetta opened a letter from the White House thanking me for volunteering to go to Vietnam. She called the University Hospital and told the operator what I had done. Annetta was shocked and angry. Word spread all over the campus, which was a hotbed of antiwar activity. Numerous students approached me and told me what they thought about the war in Vietnam. When I came home Annetta called my parents and told them what I had done. She handed me the phone and said, "Tell them what you have done." I picked up the phone and asked my mom how she was. Mom said, "I can't top that story. I don't know what to say."

Dr. Edgar Kahn, chief of neurosurgery at the University of Michigan, was very excited that I had volunteered to go to Vietnam. He was one of the very few people at the University of Michigan who supported my actions. I think he was thinking of the time he served in the U.S. Army during World War II. He called me to the OR several times to assist him in surgery, and he taught me how to put in burr holes and how to do a subtemporal decompression, which are basic neurosurgical operations particularly useful in treating trauma and battlefield injuries. While I was in Vietnam Dr. Kahn corresponded with me as well.

This was not an easy decision. I was concerned about Annetta and our two-month-old daughter, Reyna. Living in Ann Arbor, which was such an antiwar environment, worrying about Annetta and Reyna, and not knowing what the future held for me in a combat zone such as

Vietnam all contributed to a feeling of uneasiness. We finished the year at the University of Michigan after a few months and headed toward Fort Sam Houston in San Antonio, Texas, via Alabama.

CHAPTER SEVEN:
ONLY SURGEONS WIN IN WAR

Annetta, Reyna, and I drove to Montgomery, Alabama, to see my family. From there we drove over to San Antonio, Texas, for orientation into the U.S. Army. There was no housing provided for us, so we rented an apartment for two months. Annetta would stay with Reyna, and I would go to Fort Sam Houston for orientation. They taught us how to drill, how to salute, whom to salute, and all about the Army regulations. We were also measured for our uniforms. We did not have the grueling indoctrination into the military that the enlisted men experience.

From Fort Sam Houston, I was assigned to the Ninety-First Evacuation Hospital, which was temporarily located at Fort Polk, Louisiana. When we arrived at Fort Polk we were informed that there was no housing available. I think we reached one of the lowest points in our marriage when we started looking for a trailer to live in. We didn't know what the future held for us or exactly when we would be separated by my departure, and now we had no place to live. Everything seemed so depressing. While we were looking, a house opened up in a new area called New Llano, but we had no furniture. So we applied to have our furniture sent even if it was only for a month or so. While at Fort Polk, I ran the infectious diseases ward and operated with Dr. Don Pruitt, doing appendectomies and repairing perforated duodenal ulcers. We also did some orthopedic surgery.

By the end of November we were moving again, this time to Silver Spring, Maryland, for Annetta and Reyna, who was nine months old. I would be leaving Dulles Airport for Vietnam on Thanksgiving Day. Saying good-bye to Annetta and Reyna at Dulles was so difficult, even though I knew I was doing the right thing by going to war, but the times were difficult for everyone.

I was convinced that the United States was justified in getting involved in the Vietnam conflict because of the Tonkin Gulf incident. Our leaders repeatedly said that on August 2, 1964, the U.S. destroyer Maddox was fired on by three North Vietnamese boats. President Johnson convinced Congress to pass the Gulf of Tonkin Resolution, which gave him the authority to enter the war. Later we were told about the SEATO agreements in which we were obligated to defend Vietnam from advancing and encroaching Communism. Still later we were told about a domino theory, that if Vietnam was lost to Communism, other countries would follow, and it was our duty to defend them.

As the war went on, we were told we could not leave Vietnam until our 500 prisoners of war were released. Armed with the information given to the country by our leaders, I flew on to San Francisco, where I joined up with the U.S. Army. After spending a day there, I flew out to Vietnam on Continental Airlines. We stopped in Honolulu, and I sent Annetta some flowers. Then we flew to Guam for fuel, and then to the Philippines for fuel before going on to Saigon. The flight took forever, as I had a middle seat between two heavy sergeants who crowded me in my seat.

When we arrived in Saigon, they told me that they were not ready for me, so they sent me to Cam Ranh Bay at the Sixth Convalescent Center. While there we took care of American soldiers who had malaria. The rule was that if a soldier contracted malaria three times, he was sent home. Even though it was mandatory for all soldiers to take malaria pills every Monday, many did not and hoped to get malaria. Unfortunately, malaria could go to the brain, and I treated several for cerebral malaria, a disease that proved to be fatal for most of them.

There was no surgery to be done at the Sixth Convalescent Center, and after six weeks I took a helicopter ride to Tuy Hoa, where I joined up with the Ninety-First Evacuation Hospital, which had just arrived in country by ship. The hospital was to be built just off of a beach on the South China Sea. There was no village or city for at least ten miles in any direction. The hospital was built following Army directions. Initially we were in tents, but later quonset huts were built and laid out as a tropical hospital with an operating room, triage area, and personnel accommodations. Colonel Jack Maier, a radiologist, was the commanding officer, and Major Ray Smith was the executive officer, as he was a medical service officer.

Shortly after my arrival, my first patient was brought in with a gunshot wound to the abdomen. I operated on him, removed the bullet, and repaired his intestinal tract. The bullet was sent back to the USA and placed on a plaque that was then returned to Vietnam, which said something to the effect of "This is the first bullet removed from the first patient by Dr. Jack Kushner at the Ninety-First Evacuation Hospital." That plaque hung on the wall behind the chair of Colonel Maier in the headquarters. The reason that plaque had any value was that it was the first bullet removed at the hospital.

I removed the plaque a few days before I was to be rotated back to the United States, as it had some sentimental value. The Colonel called me and said he wasn't accusing me of anything, but if that plaque did not reappear, my orders to return home would be cancelled. I replaced the plaque and a few years later had occasion to meet up with one of my National Street neighbors, Dr. John Dobbins, who told me that he too was assigned to the Ninety-First Evacuation Hospital and saw the plaque. He knew then that I had been at that hospital too.

I worked with Dr. Tom Murphy, a fully trained thoracic surgeon, and Dr. Jim Alums from Texas. We worked well together and treated mostly Vietnamese and Vietcong patients. Toward the end of our stay, we received more Americans as patients. Tom realized that the only way he was going to get any sleep was to teach me how to do more surgery so that I could operate independently with a medic assistant.

A Korean Army battalion protected our hospital. One night a medevac helicopter brought in a large number of casualties and I examined these patients in the triage area. While I was examining one patient, a Korean soldier came to me and said that he wanted to talk with this patient as he was a Vietcong. The Korean took my patient out of the area to his jeep, and shortly afterward I heard a gunshot. The Korean soldier returned to tell me that the patient had tried to escape and he had to shoot him. The Vietcong were afraid of the Koreans as they had a reputation for not having many POWs to take care of.

Most of the patients we saw had wounds to their extremities, which required debridement and later a primary closure. We also had plenty of laparotomies to do and a few thoracic wounds. The head injuries were usually fatal, and we did not operate on these patients very often.

A few months later Dr. Herb Gamber and Dr. Mitch Andre joined us, and before we all rotated home, there were about twelve surgeons. Some doctors were assigned to our hospital probably by mistake, as we had an ophthalmologist, an obstetrician, and a few others who had relatively little to do, so they pitched in and assisted the surgeons. We did have a full complement of nurses, and as you can imagine, some of the doctors had their Vietnam wives, but I looked forward to receiving correspondence from Annetta.

Most of the injuries seemed to be the result of claymore mines. The soldiers had wounds in multiple areas. When exploring the intestinal tract, one would encounter intestinal parasites sticking their heads up out of the wound. There were also vascular injuries, so we repaired a lot of peripheral vessels. The liver injuries were the most difficult to treat, as we did not have any liver sutures and stopping hemorrhages was a formidable challenge. Liver surgery had not progressed at that time to the point where we could do liver repairs and transplants. Pelvic hemorrhages were also a challenge to control. I did a minimum of neurosurgery in Vietnam, except for a few peripheral nerve repairs. The head wounds were the last to pass through triage as these wounds had the least chance of survival.

Annetta did a fantastic job of sending me packages, newspapers, letters, and tapes. In fact, shortly after my arrival in Vietnam, I received a letter from her: "Dear War Hero, Where would you prefer to be buried when you get shot, as Arlington Cemetery is full?" I told her I didn't plan on getting shot or injured, so not to worry. I did arrange to see Annetta four months into my year abroad. We met in Tokyo for one week and really had an interesting time. We went sightseeing, bought Japanese art and other souvenirs, enjoyed good restaurants, and enjoyed being with each other. We saw most of the sights, including the emperor's castle and the large Buddha.

It was difficult leaving Annetta to return to Vietnam. But we saw each other again four months later. She brought Reyna with her to Hawaii, where we rented an apartment for a week. Once when we went to a Chinese restaurant, Reyna started crying, so we didn't get to eat that meal because we didn't want to disturb the other customers. But she was a good child and we had few problems with her on this trip. We all saw a lot of sights in Honolulu and enjoyed the beach. Leaving them to return to Vietnam was once again very, very difficult.

The last four months in Vietnam went by so slowly. My father wrote in August of 1967 that he knew I would be coming home soon as the leaves were beginning to fall in Alabama and I would be returning in November. And after a year, I returned home on Thanksgiving. Annetta was waiting for me at National Airport in Washington DC. We got into the car, which was stuck in a traffic jam, and it was pouring down rain. Annetta got out of the car, went to the cars ahead, and told them that she had just gotten her husband back from Vietnam and wanted to get him home, so they should move over so she could pass them. They did move over, and we were able to get out of the traffic jam and head home. I was proud of my uniform and of my Bronze Star, having been one of the very few doctors to be so decorated.

When we were at Fort Polk before I left for Vietnam, they told us we would have our choice of assignments upon returning home from Vietnam. One month prior to my return home, I received my orders to go to Fort Stewart, Georgia, without any family and without a choice of assignment. I sent a letter to Annetta and told her that it looked like we would be separated once again. Annetta called the Pentagon and some colonel answered the phone. Annetta started giving him a piece of her mind. The colonel said, "Hold it. I will call you back in a few minutes." He called back and asked Annetta if Fort Meade would be acceptable. She said she didn't know where that was, so he told her it was near Laurel, Maryland. And so I was assigned to Kimbrough Army Hospital at Fort Meade. I still had seven months to serve in the military prior to beginning my neurosurgical training at Wake Forest University in Winston-Salem, North Carolina.   When I arrived at Kimbrough Hospital at Fort Meade, they needed an orthopedic surgeon, so I was assigned as an orthopedic surgeon for the next seven months. We located an apartment in Laurel and moved there in a snowstorm with Reyna. Annetta had already contacted Blue Cross-Blue Shield about maternity care, and immediately we started working on increasing the size of our family.

It would take a few more years before I came to the conclusion that my government misled us about this war and that we probably should never have gone to war in Vietnam in the first place. Only after reading *Vietnam: A History—The First Complete Account of Vietnam at War*, by Stanley Karnow, did I understand what happened and how it all came about. By then over 58,000 American soldiers had been killed.

CHAPTER EIGHT:
NEUROSURGICAL GIANTS

Annetta, Reyna, and I arrived in Winston-Salem toward the end of June 1968. I was discharged from the military and could now resume my medical training. Initially we stayed in the Howard Johnson motel while we waited for the moving van to bring our furniture to our new house at 1925 Deborah Lane. The house was the best that we could find, but it was too small from the beginning. And by the time our second child, Eve, was born, we really were suffering from lack of space. Annetta was pregnant with Eve and was a full-time mom taking care of Reyna.

I was so happy to begin working with Dr. Eben Alexander, Dr. Courtland Davis, and Dr. David Kelly. Other residents included Dr. Ken Lassiter, Dr. John Calogero, and Dr. Richard Weiss. The program was then four years long, during which the residents evaluated the elective patients and also admit those patients who entered through the ER. We alternated our duties: one resident would spend the day in X-ray performing arteriograms, pneumoencephalograms, and myelograms, one resident would assist in surgery all day, and one would take care of the ward or floor duties such as lumbar punctures, aspirating wound hematomas, injecting chemotherapeutic agents, and writing orders to facilitate the healing process of the patients. The chief resident usually did his operations independently and was usually the first assistant for the attending most of the time, although the other residents were also first assistants as well.

Dr. Alexander could make the most routine case exciting, and after helping him you would think you had witnessed the most unusual case. Reference is made to my book *Preparing to Tack: When Physicians Change Careers*, specifically to Chapter Three, entitled "Dr. Eben Alexander." As I said in that book, his influence has been so pivotal to my thinking, my career, and my life. Although he passed away a few years ago, he left a strong neurosurgical training program and trained many neurosurgeons, who have treated many patients. Almost all of the residents thought Dr. Alexander had a great deal of charisma and sought to emulate him. He was an effective leader who was able to influence others to attain goals. He possessed power over us, but he did not need to exert it because it was not his personal style. He challenged his subordinates on a more intellectual level by using his expertise and knowledge.

Dr. Courtland Davis was educated at George Washington University and at the University of Virginia School of Medicine. After serving an internship and a residency for two years with Dr. Gayle Crutchfield at Virginia, he served in the military at Halloran General Hospital in New York and at the Walter Reed General Hospital. He then finished his residency at Duke University and worked as a senior resident with Dr. Barnes Woodhall and Dr. Guy Odom. He came to Bowman Gray School of Medicine at Wake Forest University in Winston-Salem, North Carolina, in 1952, and advanced to the position of professor of neurosurgery by 1967. Dr. Davis was active in teaching students and residents and throughout his career was active in the various committees of the North Carolina Baptist Hospital/Bowman Gray School of Medicine. He became chief of Professional Services of the North Carolina Baptist Hospital in 1982 and a member of the Faculty Executive Council of the Bowman Gray School of Medicine.

Dr. David Kelly did his residency at the North Carolina Baptist Hospital, which became the Wake Forest Medical Center. In addition, he did some of his training at Children's Hospital in Boston, Massachusetts, with Dr. Don Matson. He then did a fellowship at Washington University in neurophysiology. He was an associate professor of neurosurgery when I arrived in Winston-Salem. After I graduated from the residency program and left for Annapolis, Dr. Kelly stayed on and assumed the duties and responsibilities as chief of neurosurgery when Dr. Alexander retired. He has authored many articles for professional journals and chapters in many books. I had the honor and pleasure of working with him on four of these articles. Dr. Kelly was very instrumental in molding me as a neurosurgeon. Besides being supportive, he was an excellent teacher and surgeon.

On Tuesdays we saw patients in the clinic and reviewed our findings with the attending physician. Almost every other day all of us made rounds to see all of the patients, regardless of whose service they were on. We also frequented conferences where we discussed the various options available for treatment and the results of those options. As the years went by, we all rotated on the neurology service, the neuropathology service, and some did research. In addition to learning neurosurgery, all three attendings taught us a great deal about life and showed by example those important qualities such as honesty, integrity, and perseverance.

In our second year, Annetta and I bought a house at 1901 Robinhood Road. This was necessary as we had both Reyna and Eve, and they seemed to accumulate a lot of possessions at an early age. Because I spent so much time at the hospital, the parental duties fell on Annetta's shoulders Annetta was so busy that she did not have time to think about whether she was fulfilled. We both shared the same values with respect to education and stressed this from the very beginning. The children were started in Montessori School at age three.

The requirements of the residency were an improvement over George Washington University Hospital, as I was able to spend nights at home, even though I had to return to the ER to see patients on my nights on duty and to the hospital to take care of any problems with patients there. At the end of the third year, I passed the written part of the neurosurgical board examination. I took the exam again for practice at the end of my fourth year.

I felt secure enough to leave the residency program in 1972 and start out on my own in Annapolis at the Anne Arundel General Hospital. This location was actually identified by my brother-in-law, Dr. Norman Horwitz, who practiced neurosurgery in Washington DC at the Washington Hospital Center and at George Washington University Hospital. Norman facilitated my obtaining hospital privileges at the Washington Hospital Center. When our time in North Carolina was finished, Annetta sold our house and we packed up and left for Annapolis, Maryland. Reyna was six, Eve was four, so we looked for schools for both of them as soon as we arrived in Annapolis.

CHAPTER NINE:
NEUROSURGERY WHERE GEORGE WASHINGTON RESIGNED HIS COMMISSION

Perhaps the third most important document in American history is located in Annapolis, Maryland. For it was on December 23, 1783, that George Washington resigned his commission before the Senate at the then-U.S. Capitol of the United States. While reading the original resignation speech, Washington struck out "an affectionate final farewell to this august body" and substituted "an affectionate farewell to this august body."

By any standards of history, he might have said that since he was the commanding officer, he would stay on as the military chief of the USA or some other lifelong position. Instead, he reverted all power that he possessed as commanding officer back to the Congress—such as it was at that time. He was the American version of Lucius Quinctius Cincinnatus, the Roman general who left the military and returned to civilian life in 458 BCE. After Washington resigned his commission, he had lunch at Londontown and then continued his trip home to Mount Vernon. Because of the beauty and the history of Annapolis, we were attracted to this city and have been here ever since.

Prior to coming to Annapolis, I had submitted a list of the surgical equipment I would need to practice neurosurgery, and I prioritized the list. One of the items I listed was an OR table on which the instruments would be placed. I was amused when I arrived to learn that the nurses had never seen such a table. They thought that somehow I was going to place the patient on the table, which was not the case. In addition, there was no pneumoencephalogram chair, no automatic plate changer for arteriograms, and no brain scan. There was competition for beds in the hospital among the physicians and surgeons, and there was significant competition for operating room space. There were four operating rooms and an additional room for urological procedures. There were four anesthesiologists. I was the forty-second doctor on the staff, and everyone knew each other. There was no other neurosurgeon. A full-time neurologist, a medical specialist who diagnoses nonsurgical diseases and conditions that affect the nervous system but does not perform any surgical procedures, would arrive the following year.

A doctor in Baltimore ran an itinerant EEG and echoencephalogram service and would send a technician to Annapolis for these tests. One of the first controversies I encountered was on this very issue. Dr. Schilder wanted the hospital to purchase an EEG, and if the hospital did so, then it would lose the echoencephalogram service. Since at that time I was the one who used the echoencephalogram service for patients with head injuries in the ER, I objected to the new plan to install an EEG and I ruffled feathers. In retrospect, it probably would have been better in the long run if I had not objected, because in time we would have an echoencephalogram, a CAT scan, and better angiography to detect cerebral hemorrhage.

I was extremely busy as I was the only neurosurgeon. I went to the ER to see consults at least twice every twenty-four hours, sometimes even more often. I was on call every day and every night, and it took its toll on me. Our children were in school, and Annetta was busy doing most of the parenting duties. In addition to seeing patients in the office, I did numerous X-ray studies, including myelograms, pneumoencephalograms, and arteriograms. I did several operations every day and emergency surgery in the evenings and on weekends.

Since we did not have a house staff, all of the surgeons participated as assistant surgeons to each other. This was always a problem, because having an obstetrician assist on a neurosurgical procedure was not helpful, nor was it helpful to have an elderly physician assist who did not know anything about neurosurgery. But that was the way it was, and I had to deal with this adversity.

As time went on, the space competition in the OR became more acute, and I found myself doing elective surgery commencing at 8 PM night after night. In order to rectify this situation, I ran for a seat on the board of managers and was elected. This enabled me to ameliorate the situation to some extent but put me in an uncomfortable position on another issue. In addition to the above, I was given an academic position at the Johns Hopkins Medical Center, at George Washington University, and at the Washington Hospital Center in Washington DC. I passed the oral exam in neurosurgery and became certified by the American Board of Neurosurgery.

When the Anne Arundel Hospital was young, they had difficulty attracting board-certified specialists. In order to attract radiologists, the hospital bent over backward to accommodate them. In fact, the hospital provided space for the Radiology Department, provided the X-ray machines and all associated equipment, radiology technicians, secretarial support, and the personnel for billing and insurance. But as the years went by, it became much easier for the hospital to attract certified physicians, and the hospital administration started thinking that it should be run more like a business. The board of managers initiated a plan whereby a new Department of Imaging would be created, and the hospital would share the profits from that department. Bills would go out to the patients stating that there was a hospital component and a physician service component. The hospital would own all of the equipment and would share future acquisition costs with the doctors.

A search was made for a new chief of Imaging, and Dr. Barry Friedman was selected. He in turn fired all of the existing radiologists and brought in new radiologists. Immediately lawsuits were filed, with doctors suing each other and the hospital. This controversy went on for two years and made serving on the board of managers and being on the Medical Staff uncomfortable, as they were sympathetic to the original radiologists. After numerous depositions and court appearances, the controversy was settled, and Dr. Barry Friedman was released and replaced by Dr. Vernon Croft. Shortly thereafter I resigned from the board of managers.

One of the more interesting events at the hospital involved the acquisition of the CAT scanner. The state of Maryland health care planners felt that we did not need a CAT scanner in Annapolis and that we could send our patients to Baltimore to either the University of Maryland Hospital or Johns Hopkins Hospital. I attended numerous hearings on this subject and argued that we needed a CAT scanner for emergencies and could not be sending sick patients to Baltimore. Finally the state planners agreed, and I had to sign a document promising that I would send at least five patients a week for this study. I think now in 2009 we have about five CAT scanners in the city and more in the county.

A few years later, when the MRI scanner became available, we had to repeat the scenario and again go to hearings with the state planners. Our hospital was allowed to purchase the MRI scanner, but because of lack of space the MRI was located across town, where the new hospital would be built. This would prove to be a problem: we had to transport sick patients by ambulance to the MRI, stay with them, and bring them back with all their supporting equipment, such as respirators, ventricular drainage tubes, IV tubes, and Foley catheters. Now the hospital has two MRI scanners that operate on a full schedule.

In 1977 another neurosurgeon came to town. Dr. N. Kitrinos worked with me for about five years until he had a fatal heart attack. Although we had some personality problems, it was an advantage to having a neurosurgeon assist in surgery and cover the hospital for me when I went out of town. Dr. Tom Ducker, whom I had met as a resident at the University of Michigan, replaced Dr.Kitrinos.

While practicing in Annapolis, I encountered many interesting cases. One of the more gratifying cases was that of Mr. Robin Woolford. Robin was eighteen years old and was working at the cleaners on West Street in Annapolis. One night a robber entered the cleaners and demanded that Robin hand over the money in the cash register, which he did. Unfortunately, the robber shot Robin in the neck and the bullet caused a significant spinal cord concussion. I operated on Robin, removed the bullet, and repaired the dura mater. Postoperatively, Robin gradually regained the movement in his extremities and learned to walk with a cane.

Recently I saw Robin's picture in the local paper; he was lecturing to criminals in prison. He spoke about how much collateral damage occurs when crimes are committed. This particular crime significantly altered his life, but Robin has made a huge comeback He was able to commute from Annapolis to Washington DC and attend George Washington University. He earned a bachelor's degree in international relations with a minor in Russian. Then he worked in the mortgage business for many years, but for the past eight years he has been the director of the Maryland Criminal Injuries Compensation Board, providing a certain amount of compensation to victims of crime as an insurer of last resort. He has three children. This was a most satisfying case, and I am proud of the recovery Robin has made and the life he has led despite the serious setback that would have devastated others.

Several other cases stand out in my mind. Patient Number Two was a thirty-eight-year-old woman over eight months pregnant who entered the hospital with a severe headache. Further evaluation revealed that she had a posterior communicating artery aneurysm on the right side of her head. I scheduled her for a craniotomy and made arrangements for an obstetrician (OB) and an obstetrical nurse to be in the operating room monitoring the fetus. I was able to clip her aneurysm, and there was no need for the OB assistance that day. A few weeks later she delivered a nine-pound boy. Both the patient and the baby did well without any complications.

Patient Number Three was a fifty-five-year-old male who entered the Annapolis hospital with a severe headache. Evaluation revealed that he had a frontal lobe arteriovenous malformation, which had bled. I scheduled him for a craniotomy, during which we were able to remove the malformation. This was a most challenging case, as an arteriovenous malformation can be very difficult to treat. This is an abnormal collection of vessels and can be located in an eloquent section of the brain that controls speech or motor function. He made an uneventful recovery.

Patient Number Four was an eighteen-year-old co-ed from St. John's College in Annapolis. She had gone to the nearby shopping area and walked back to her dormitory around 7 PM. Apparently someone followed her right into the dorm and attacked her. She was brought to the ER with seven compound depressed skull fractures. I elevated these fractures and she was able to return to school shortly thereafter.

Patient Number Five was an eighteen-year-old midshipman from the U.S. Naval Academy who developed an epidural hematoma after participating in boxing class. I scheduled him for surgery immediately and evacuated the hematoma, and he was able to return to class shortly thereafter and matriculate with his class.

Patient Number Six: While a resident neurosurgeon at Wake Forest Medical, I once treated a patient who had been attacked with a meat cleaver. The foreign instrument was still in the head, transecting both frontal lobes of the brain. Despite all efforts, we had difficulty controlling the hemorrhage and the patient did not survive. Years later in Annapolis, I saw a patient with a machete transecting the frontal lobes of the brain. This time I was more prepared for the situation and removed the weapon only when we were ready to stop the hemorrhaging. This patient survived. There are many more interesting cases, but I cannot describe them all.

My disillusionment with the practice of neurosurgery increased as the malpractice insurance premiums grew. The number of malpractice suits also grew all over the country. Initially doctors could increase their fees to cover the growing malpractice insurance premiums, but with the growth of health maintenance organizations (HMOs), the reimbursement rates declined each year, as did the Medicare reimbursement rates. In addition, the government mandated that all doctors increase their overhead by hiring personnel to monitor the billing process and to ensure accurate billing of third-party payers. Later the government mandated that all offices employ someone to ensure that the privacy laws were upheld and that no health care information about a patient left the office unless the patient signed documents attesting to permission.

As these forces increased, I did not know what the future held, but I enrolled at the University of Maryland University College in the master's program for finance in September 1987 at the age of forty-eight. I wasn't sure where I was headed, but I sensed that I was going to leave medicine for some other career and that I would reinvent myself. Most of the classes were initially at the United States Naval Academy in the evening. At first I took only one class a semester, because I didn't know how I would do with courses such as accounting, which required computer skills. Later I was concerned about my ability to write research papers and utilize the library, and I wasn't sure I could still memorize lists of important information.

In 1989 I started taking two courses each semester, and my final courses were taught only at the University of Maryland campus in College Park. I attended all of my classes with my beeper and telephone. Sometimes I would leave class, go to the hospital, see a consult, and return to the lecture. When I was up at midnight trying to work on accounting problems, I often asked myself what I was doing and why I was doing it.

My last semester at the University of Maryland required that I write another paper. In my previous years at the University of Maryland when I wrote papers, I relied on my wife, who was an adjunct professor of English at Washington College, to visit their library and obtain any papers or books that I required. By this time my wife had retired from teaching and declined to make the trip to the Eastern shore city of Chestertown to access their library in my behalf. Instead, she insisted that I should know where the library at the University of Maryland was before I graduated. I said that was fine with me, closed my office early, and drove over to College Park.

After I parked I walked to the library and looked for the references. I was unable to find any of them, so I went to the desk to see the librarian. Some young college kid with his hat on backward and his shoes untied said, "Mister, you have to get in line." I got in line, waited my turn, and finally got to the desk. I gave my list of references to the librarian, who examined them and pronounced that I was at the wrong library. After he gave me directions, I walked across campus to another library and once again looked for my references. And once again, I could not find anything. This time I got in line, waited my turn, and got to the librarian. I gave her my list and she looked at them. Then she said, "Mister, you have to fill out a card for each one of the references."

I said, "Give me the cards," and I started filling them out at the counter in front of her.

She said, "No, mister, you have to go to another desk to fill out the cards, then return them to me."

So I went and filled out twenty cards and returned to the librarian. I asked where my books were, and she said the way the library worked was that they would mail them to me the next day. Upon returning to my car I found a parking ticket.

The next day the mail brought back all of my cards and none of the references. The cards were stamped with a note saying that I was not eligible for the library as I was not a full-time student. I made several phone calls and it was determined that in fact I was eligible to use the library. The next week I returned, picked up my books, and got another parking ticket. I am told now that I would never have to go to the library because everything is online.

During this time our children had gotten older, and we had to make some decisions about their education. We were not satisfied that Key School satisfied their needs, so we sent them to Choate Rosemary Hall in Wallingford, Connecticut, for their high school years. Reyna went on to Wellesley College and got her post-graduate education in theoretical nuclear physics at George Washington University. Eve went on to Dartmouth and studied creative writing and English.

In 1988, prior to my completing my master's degree in general administration in the financial track, I started a company called Transcriptions International. The idea behind this venture was that medical transcription was a necessary item, but it was difficult to obtain transcriptionists. Transcriptionist training required computer skills, a working knowledge of medical vocabulary in many different specialties, and some knowledge of insurance company policies and billing. If they had all of these skills, usually they could find an occupation that paid better than transcription.

My plan was to electronically transmit the dictation of the operating notes, the history and physical exams, and the various reports from the radiologist and the pathologist to India, where medical transcriptionists could type the material and send it back. I had tried some transcriptionists in the Dominican Republic who were bilingual, but that just did not work out because of the nuances in the languages. Initially we tried working with CNN with the satellite system since they were using their equipment twelve hours a day until the first Persian Gulf War. Later we were able to work with the Internet, which was much better and cheaper.

Dealing with the workers in India presented many problems. For example, the employer could hardly fire an employee in India, which meant once the employer hired them he had to retain them even if they were not competent. In addition, there were many restrictions, as we were one of the first to start outsourcing business to India. We spent a lot of our resources developing the computer that would transmit dictation to India and receive it electronically, and then we redistributed it to various places such as hospitals and doctors' offices.

Although I left the company in 1991 and was no longer involved with the day-to-day operations, the company was in good hands with Skip Conover and proceeded to grow. The company was sending out dictation for typing in India and also added medical billing, accounting, typesetting for the printing industry, and a telephone call center, thereby igniting the revolution of business process outsourcing services to India, which is now a $15 billion industry.

Over the years, Transcriptions International morphed into CBay Systems and Services, which is still a large contributor to employment in the Annapolis area and was named Tech Company of the Year in 2005. Now, as a result of our vision, more than 25,000 Indian medical transcriptionists are gainfully employed today. The Government of India tells us that each job provides economic activity to feed ten Indians. It can be reasonably stated that our vision contributed substantially to the lives of hundreds of thousands of people throughout the world.

In 1993, while I was still practicing neurosurgery, I was invited by Oppenheimer Company to go with a group to Israel to see some of the companies they had taken public. This turned out to be a pivotal trip, as the names of companies I had heard about now had names and faces associated with them. Twelve interested persons went on the trip with five employees of Oppenheimer, including the president. We were given several lectures on the thriving start-up business development in Israel.

After the didactic lectures, we traveled throughout Israel to visit these companies and see the people running them. I was particularly impressed with a company that used virtual reality to teach pilots how to fly, soldiers how to use artillery, and others how to drive tanks during warfare. That is where I got the idea that we could use virtual reality to teach surgeons how to operate, teach anesthesiologists how to manage critical care patients, and teach various medical procedures, such as colonoscopy. I also saw a group of people working on a capsule with a camera inside that could take pictures of the intestinal tract as the capsule moves along the gastrointestinal tract.

I saw other companies that were doing interesting things with VSAT devices (satellite transmission) and lots of high tech work for computers and cell phones. Most of the workers had served their time in the military, had gone on to university, and now were starting out in the high tech industry. I became very enthusiastic about the world I had visited and thought surely there were ways to utilize this information in medicine and surgery. This country was just one huge incubator coming out with new ideas, new products, and new concepts. Entrepreneurship was the order of the day.

Armed with a master's degree in general administration in the financial track (1990) and some experience in business with Transcriptions International (1988), my disillusionment with the future of delivering health care influenced me to make the decision to start a new career. I had seen other doctors wringing their hands, stating that they only had five more years and then they would be out of medicine. Or I saw them in the doctors' lounge saying that they planned to retire soon. I did not want to wish away my life, nor did I want to continue doing something I no longer enjoyed. The way medicine was evolving was not the life I had chosen many years ago. I felt that a career that involved technology, combined with the ideas and dreams of entrepreneurs, was exciting, even if it was uncertain. So I started making plans to leave medicine and to work in a new field in July 1995.

Just as I was planning to leave, I was hit with a malpractice suit concerning a carotid endarterectomy and with a complaint concerning an emergency room disposition in which I referred a patient to Johns Hopkins for the treatment of an unusual brain tumor. Because I did not call ahead and had sent the parents and the patient on to the Johns Hopkins ER, a complaint was filed for unprofessional conduct.

The town newspaper splashed a big story about my leaving medicine for virtual reality technology and then a few weeks later concluded that the reason I was leaving was because of the above. Three years later, when I won the malpractice suit, I asked the newspaper to write another article clearing my name, but they claimed that people had forgotten all about it and were no longer interested in the story. The other complaint was essentially dropped in view of the fact that no harm came to the patient and I was leaving medicine anyway. No hearing was ever conducted, and thus no negative finding was ever determined. It was unfortunate that these accusations arose, but no malfeasance was ever proven or determined.

I then proceeded to continue with my interest in the financial aspects of business. Our children were married by then. Annetta was not very happy about my leaving medicine.

In addition to changes in my professional life, my parents were beginning to suffer the ravages of aging. When my father had a seizure later in life, we sent him to the University Hospital in Birmingham. While he was getting an EEG, the technician said to him "Mr. Kushner, what is wrong with you? You don't look sick."

My father responded, "I sent two boys to medical school and one to law school, and now they think I need to have my head examined."

CHAPTER TEN:
TACKING: CHANGING CAREERS

Word of my leaving medicine disseminated to the American College of Surgery. I was pleased to be invited by the College to become a member of the Committee of Emerging Technology. I told them about my experiences with medical transcription and my ideas about teaching surgery with surgical simulation. I also had ideas about telemedicine, a way for patients from all over the world to consult with expert American doctors. Everyone else on this committee was a professor of his or her surgical specialty and chairman of the respective department. I was the only one who wasn't even practicing surgery any longer, so I really was proud of this appointment.

I then proceeded to travel all over the world looking for people and companies who could manufacture a virtual reality surgical simulator with which we could teach. I worked with Dr. Richard Satava, who had been with DARPA (a Department of Defense research agency), and Dr. J. Carrico, who was also on the Committee of Emerging Technology. We had a demonstration simulator on exhibit at several of the meetings held by the American College of Surgeons. We envisioned simulator centers at every medical center so that surgeons could gain proficiency performing new operations. We saw this educational technique evolving with the use of virtual reality technology and various mannequins.

Although we received support from most general surgeons and from hospitals, we did not receive much encouragement from one of the neurosurgical leaders who considered himself to be a guru of technology. This particular neurosurgeon wrote denigrating articles about the future of this technology, which had the effect of slowing down the progress of surgical simulation, particularly in neurosurgery. Although everyone was interested, I had difficulty finding anyone with the proficiency and expertise to manufacture this equipment at a reasonable price. I visited animation companies and companies that did work in this field for the U.S. military in the Baltimore-Washington-Virginia area, in Boston, Evans and Sutherland in Salt Lake City, in Ames, Iowa, in California, and in Texas. I also went to Singapore, Stockholm, Germany, and England.

I returned to Israel with Dr. Jim Ausman, chief of neurosurgery at the University of Illinois at Chicago, who was very interested in this technology and was editor of *Surgical Neurology*. I also had an interesting visit with Uzia Galil, the CEO of Elron Electronics in Israel. His question was who my customer would be. Surely, I thought, everyone would want a simulator. His point was that his company had manufactured a CAT scanner and a MRI, and all of the medical schools and university hospitals wanted these machines to be gifted to them. He warned me that none of them would want to actually buy these machines. At the time I did not think he was right and continued to speak at many universities and medical schools about the advantages of teaching with simulation.

I spoke at Johns Hopkins Medical School, University of Pennsylvania, Penn State, University of Alabama Medical School, University of Illinois at Chicago, Wake Forest University Medical School, University of Maryland Medical School, University of South Carolina Medical School, University of Utah Medical School, Iowa

State University Department of Engineering, Stanford University Department of Computer Science, George Washington University Medical School, and a few others. Most of them said they were interested but could not make a decision at that time and wanted me to return and speak to yet another committee. They talked about the fact that their budget was fixed for a year or so, that they did not want to deal with a learning curve that would require them to teach all of their personnel, and that they wanted to wait until the technology was more mature. George Washington University Medical School was working in this space already and did not know who actually owned the work that was done; i.e., whether it belonged to the anatomy department, the surgery department, or the engineering department.

I also approached many of the financial institutions that are now in dire straits or out of business. They told me that this surgical simulation concept was too speculative for them to consider an investment. Apparently these institutions did not think mortgage-backed derivatives were more speculative than surgical simulators. I invested in several simulators dealing with critical care management but later sold them to a company in Florida that was a distributor.

Years later, after I had abandoned this effort for lack of funding, I received a call from someone at Johns Hopkins University Medical School saying they were going to build a simulation center and were looking for contributions. I told them I was there with this issue fifteen years ago and they were not interested. Now almost every medical center has a simulator. Tulane University School of Medicine has the most advanced surgical simulation laboratory in the world and has connected this technology with an innovative concept called "Team Training" or crew resource management. I was ahead of my time, but I am glad that the technology has finally found its place in medicine. I have been involved in other technical applications.

Telemedicine has a lot of definitions and applications. When a patient talks with a doctor about his condition on the telephone or via e-mail, that is telemedicine. We worked with several applications of this concept. My first contact with this technology in an advanced mode was with a company in Israel in 1997. An insurance company and a credit card company funded this particular company. The global insurance company paid the telemedicine company in advance on a capitation basis. Every client of the insurance company was entitled to a free second opinion with an American doctor if he had an insurance policy such as a homeowner's policy, an auto insurance policy, or even a workman's compensation policy. A rider in the insurance policy gave the client this privilege.

Arrangements were made in advance with four American medical centers so that the clients could have an unlimited number of consultations. The client from a foreign country had his medical records sent to Israel for translation purposes and then they were sent electronically to a medical center in the USA, where an arrangement for payment purposes had been made in advance. If the doctor needed to see the patient, a teleconference and videoconference was then arranged. The insurance company used this telemedicine agreement as a marketing tool and really didn't care just how many clients used this option.

A variation of this application is an arrangement where a telemedicine center is established and various smaller spin-off branches are established. Then a nurse or a physician's assistant can examine the patient in the spin-off facility, and a doctor at the university medical center will see exactly what the assistant sees with telemedicine equipment. The otoscope or the ophthalmoscope is set up so that whatever is visualized by the examiner is transmitted to the medical center for a completely trained and qualified doctor to see. This procedure allows a medical center to provide medical care to rural areas that are distant from the medical center. This technology also applies to X-rays and other studies such as blood CAT scans and EKGs. In addition, doctors at a medical center can monitor patients in the intensive care units in hospitals in rural areas where the doctors are not physically in the hospitals twenty-four hours a day. This is a variation of telemedicine.

Another application deals with the reading of X-rays, CAT scans, MRIs, and mammograms via telemedicine. This can be done across national borders and oceans and is helpful when there is a time difference. In this way hospitals can have access to radiologists twenty-four hours a day, even when the radiologists are miles away.

Still another variation in which we invested was home care. A patient can sit in front of his computer or television and be seen by a health care professional. A wound can be visualized and questions can be answered. This permits the patient to leave the hospital sooner yet be in the constant care of a health care professional.

All of these techniques are components of our interest in giving more power to the patient, i.e., to move toward patient-driven communication and medical orientation. Presently, the invisible third party that pays for health care is making the medical decisions in most of the cases. This needs to be changed so that every person is in charge of his or her health destiny.

We worked on a plan and a system so that the patients could access the most expert specialists in various medical disciplines. We tried to market this as a benefit or an affinity product for other companies. Although there was some interest from some of the banks, we were not successful in integrating this system into the maze of health care programs.

In business, one does not always have to be the entrepreneur, the inventor, or the CEO of a new concept. I have always felt that investment is also a good way to participate in various business activities. One of the ways in which I participated was to attend the young Startup Ventures established by Mr. Joe Benjamin in New York and Boston. Another aspect of this forum is the Corporate Venture Capital Summit. These meetings present opportunities for start-up businesses to show their wares before venture capital companies and investors. Most of these companies are small companies from Israel and are seeking funding, and many of them have interesting ideas that will prove to be something of value.

In addition to meeting these companies in the USA, I frequently went to Israel and interviewed numerous companies with the idea of making investments. This was facilitated by Dr. Yves Bitton in Tel Aviv, who usually arranged for these companies to meet with me. Dr. Bitton has a long history of innovating improvements in health care. As a medical student he helped incorporate the teaching of health care to high school students in Israel. He originated the idea of getting second opinions via telemedicine and has also developed several methods of increasing the feasibility of home health care, including the development of health care on wheels.

As time went on, the idea arose to not just invest money in these firms, but to bring them to the USA, connect them with an American company in the same field, and get paid by accepting a certain percentage of stock. Some financial event would have to occur before we would ever realize any benefit or reward.

I started American Opportunity Portal with the intent to identify companies abroad and bring them to the USA to create jobs. We started looking at these companies by examining each one's proprietary product and the history of sales of that product. Hopefully the product was accompanied with a patent or copyright. We sought several types of affiliations for companies coming to the USA. We could strive to arrange a merger or acquisition, a joint venture, a partnership, a subcontractor, a distributor agent or representative, an affiliated partner, or an independent contractor.

We examined the relationship by asking questions such as "What makes affiliations work? What makes affiliations have serious problems?" Then we would see just what competitive advantages these companies had and scan the horizon for new markets and new customers. We would see just what complementary products were available. Then we would compose an operating agreement and stress what liabilities there were, what obligations and limitations the new company would have, what the ownership issues were, and just what compensation each person in the new company would have. We then concentrated on the due diligence, oversight and governance, financial and legal issues. Then we considered just what could go wrong. We were more than interested in value leakage, accountability, and customer feedback. Finally, we completed a marketing plan, a current business development plan, and a budget.

During our involvement in these business activities, other opportunities arose, such as technology transfer from various universities. When I visited the University of Sheffield in England, Professor Bob Boucher introduced me to several of their inventions and encouraged me to bring them to the USA to increase the marketing exposure. Then we examined some of those inventions emanating from Tulane University, where I was director at large of the Tulane Alumni Association. From there I visited and made several trips to Wake Forest University, where I did my neurosurgical training years ago. Wake Forest University has one of the best facilities for research and has been attracting a large number of research scientists. There are large companies specializing in technology transfer, but in view of the fact that we at American Opportunity Portal and Bottom-Line Partners have been working with a large number of diversified companies, opportunities arise from such networking.

My association with Mr. Jim Handlon of Bottom-Line Partners has resulted in interviewing a large number of companies. We were involved in making good corporations great and great corporations outstanding. We strove to partner with companies in order to drive results. We identified growth opportunities and implemented goals. We focused on top-line acceleration and bottom-line results by providing high-horsepower talent and executives. Since we were accountable for delivering results, we would share in the success. Our company would take equity as part of the arrangement, and we would create a winning strategy and lead its implementation. In addition to working with established companies, we also worked with international startups.

Besides looking for capital for the Israeli companies, we worked with a new fish bait company, a gynecological medical device company, a new soft drink company, and a nuclear-powered electric company. One of the more interesting projects was the attempted purchase of Columbus University in Panama City, Panama. Dr. Villar wanted to sell the medical school, and in order for this purchase to make financial sense, we would have to build a larger medical school. Arrangements were made to build such a facility at the old Howard Air Force Base, which the USA had gifted to Panama when the USA turned over the Panama Canal. While we were looking for funding, some other group bought it from under us but ran into the same problem we did with the credit crunch, which has affected the world. We probably were lucky to have not started construction on the new facility, because the lending institution might have stopped the funding right in the middle of the construction, which would have left us holding the loan with nothing to show for it.

CHAPTER ELEVEN:
LEADING UP TO HALL OF FAME

I have been very fortunate and honored in my life. While I was practicing neurosurgery, I was elected to the board of managers at the Anne Arundel Hospital and received the Community Leaders of America Award. After I started practice in Annapolis, I was invited to give a paper to the Israeli Obstetrical Association on depressed skull fractures in the newborn. A few years later I was invited to give a speech to the Society of British Neurological Surgeons about the brainstem findings on a CAT scan at Cork University in Ireland. I was invited to speak on two occasions to the Galil Telemedicine Institute at the Technion University in Haifa, Israel. In May 2009 I was invited to lecture at the University of Zagreb in Croatia. I also gave several neurosurgical papers to the various American neurosurgical organizations.

I was proud to be certified by the American Board of Neurological Surgery. I appreciated being invited to attend the Twenty-Eighth Air War College Symposium in 1978, which was an interesting experience. While there, several selected civilians met with military officers to discuss the foreign policy of the United States and how this policy might affect the military.

I was elected to the American Association of Neurological Surgeons, the Congress of Neurological Surgeons, the Southern Neurosurgical Society, and the American College of Surgeons, the International

College of Surgeons, the Royal Society of Medicine, the New York Academy of Science, the Pan-Pacific Surgical Association, and the American Academy of Medical Directors. In 2001 I was honored by the University College of Maryland and was named the Most Distinguished Alumnus. Later I was honored by the International Biographical Centre (IBC) with a Lifetime Achievement Award and by the American Biographical Institute as the Man of the Year in 2004.

I have been listed in numerous books, such as *Men of Achievement, 2000 Outstanding People of the 20th Century*, Strathmore's *Who's Who*, and Marquis *Who's Who in America, Who's Who in the World, Who's Who in the East*, and *Who's Who in Finance and Business*. I was named in the Top 100 Health Professionals by the IBC in 2005 and America's Top Surgeons in 2002, and I presently serve as director at large of the Tulane University Alumni Association.

I also received the Marie Curie Award from the International Biographical Centre at St. Catherine's College at Oxford University, followed by the Lifetime Achievement Award and the Hall of Fame Award, which was also presented at Oxford University. Along with serving on the Committee of Emerging Technology with the American College of Surgeons, I served on the Military Leadership Circle for the University of Maryland. I have published numerous articles in peer-reviewed medical journals and am the author of *Preparing to Tack: When Physicians Change Careers.*

Chapter Twelve:
Green Wave and Midshipmen

I have enjoyed my association with the various universities. I have been extremely active with The Tulane University Alumni Association since just prior to the time when Hurricane Katrina hit New Orleans and caused a great deal of damage to the university. When I was inducted into the Hall of Fame at Oxford University, I spoke about this problem in detail. I explained to the audience that in August 2005 Hurricane Katrina devastated the entire city of New Orleans, flooding more than half of Tulane's uptown campus and all of its downtown Health Sciences Center.

President Scott Cowen felt it was his duty to stay and ride the hurricane out after everyone was safely evacuated. Initially after the hurricane came through, he looked out the window and saw tree branches everywhere. The next morning he looked out the window and saw only water everywhere—eight feet deep. The landlines did not work. The cell phones did not work. The only thing that worked was a vibration he felt in his pocket, as people were able to send text messages, but he wasn't certain as to how to access the text messages.

He teamed up with a maintenance man who had also stayed through the hurricane. They searched all the rooms and drawers in some of the buildings looking for food but only located some cookies and potato chips. Under the student recreation center the two of them located an old rowboat. Together they were able to take the steering wheel off of an automobile, hook it to the rowboat, and siphon gasoline from an automobile and use it for the rowboat engine, which they connected. They were able to sail down St. Charles Avenue to the downtown area to see who was still there and what the damage might be. The next day, President Scott Cowen was evacuated by helicopter and left for Houston, Texas.

In Houston, several of the administrators gathered in his hotel room. They did not have any financial records, academic records, or any kind of record showing who was a student or a professor at Tulane University. Indeed, there was no university at that moment, only a virtual one in their minds. They did not know how they were going to pay their staff or the professors, nor did they know where all the students were.

As it turned out, the students were placed in five hundred colleges and universities across the country. An arrangement was made that allowed Tulane to keep the tuitions paid, and the various universities would charge neither Tulane nor the students for one semester. The other universities agreed not to officially accept any of the Tulane students for transfer until they eventually returned to Tulane as a student. Many professors sought refuge at other universities.

We at Tulane University did not have a blueprint or a road map to rebuild the university. The only example of a university being so completely destroyed was the University of Alabama, when the Northern troops burned the university, but that university was a state-funded public university and Tulane is private. While some in the group started working on recreating the lists of students, professors, and staff, others started thinking about acquiring funding to rebuild the university. Within a few weeks, the damage was estimated to be about $600 million, as eighty-four buildings had to be renovated.

Some of us worked with our contacts in New York, and we were able to get a loan for $700 million from a European bank for one point below LIBOR (the London Interbank Offered Rate on Eurodollar deposits traded between banks). The administration started working on reorganizing the university, combining some offices in administration, and discontinuing some courses and departments that were not revenue enhancers. Three engineering programs were discontinued, and a new Science and Engineering Department was created. Newcomb College for women was combined with Tulane University College of Arts and Sciences and Tulane College. Every student was required to spend time rebuilding the community and the university. In addition, it became necessary to mandate that all freshmen and sophomores live in the Tulane dormitories.

The board of directors approved President Scott Cowen's Renewal Plan. A remarkable 93 percent of the students returned in January 2006. In 2007 Tulane had a large increase in the number of applications, which reached 35,000, and the next year it increased to 40,000 applicants for 1,500 spaces. Now, in 2009, Tulane has repaid all but $100 million of the loan already.

Once when I was giving a speech about Tulane and the recovery from Hurricane Katrina, I rambled on and on about how great a university Tulane is and spoke about the numerous graduates who have distinguished themselves in every field. I mentioned that Tulane was founded in 1834. When I finished speaking, someone in the audience raised his hand and said, "I am from Krakow, Poland, and attended university in that city. That particular university was founded in the twelfth century, and one of their alumni was Copernicus." I told him I could not compete with that information but appreciated having our alumni compared to Copernicus.

I have continued my association with the University of Sheffield. Every year we have a dinner in New York for Sheffield in America. I have returned to Sheffield, England, for a reunion and for the Kroto Research Symposium, named after Sir Harry Kroto, who received the Nobel Prize in Chemistry. I have discussed with the Vice Chancellor of the Sheffield University the possibility of marketing some of their inventions in the United States.

Because I have lived in Annapolis, Maryland, since 1972, I have become involved in several activities at the United States Naval Academy. I participated in the fundraising for the new Uriah P. Levy Center and support the Distinguished Arts Program. I have operated on a few midshipmen through the years who have sustained injuries. I belong to the U.S. Naval Academy Golf Association and served as tournament director for the senior golfers. I am a member of the Officers' and Faculty Club.

One of the most satisfying moments in my working relationship with the U.S. Naval Academy was when I brought two Nobel laureates to the Academy as guest speakers. When I was a student at the University of Sheffield, Harry Kroto was a friend who lived at Crewe Hall. We often played tennis. I lost contact with Harry but became reunited with him at a Sheffield reunion and supported a sculpture at the new Kroto Research Center. After he won the Nobel Prize in Chemistry, I arranged for him to visit the Naval Academy as a guest speaker. I met Sir Richard Roberts at a Sheffield in America meeting and also arranged for him to speak at the Naval Academy with the help of Dr. Chris Kinter, professor of chemistry at the Academy. Both of these Nobel laureates gave wonderful lectures, and everyone appreciated their visits. They will also speak at Tulane University.

CHAPTER THIRTEEN:
SOLOMONICALLY WISE DECISIONS

As I write this book, the times do not seem a great deal better or worse than they were for my parents back in 1939. We may be on the verge of another Great Depression, and Israel has just finished another war in their series of wars. Iran will acquire nuclear weapons within a year and has threatened the very existence of Israel. Iran launched a satellite into space just the other day. We have a new, untested president who has so many problems with which to deal. We all have a great deal of hope that President Barack Obama can solve some of these problems, and we wish him well.

As I look back on my life, I made two really difficult decisions that really affected my life and the lives of my family. One was the decision to go to Vietnam when I didn't have to, and the other was to leave medicine when I had worked all my life to get into that profession. I think in retrospect that you have to come to grips with who you are and what you believe in. With regard to the first decision, I knew that I was a partially trained surgeon and that I was educated in the treatment of tropical diseases. I knew that my country was at war, rightly or wrongly, but my friends and others were being sent to a combat zone. It was not in my genetic makeup to even consider sitting the war out by hiding in Virginia and Greenland. I was married with a child and had a responsibility to them. But over one million Americans went to Vietnam, and more had defended this country in previous wars, and many of them had families back home. In fact, in World War II, the soldiers were in the military for the duration of the war as opposed to the one-year tour of duty we had. And so after evaluating the various points, I decided to go to Vietnam. I was fortunate to not be injured and to return home to my family and commence working on my career.

My daughter has expressed her concern about our country and the military and wants to protect her son from ever having to go to war. She has expressed an opinion that she might consider moving to Canada if we reinstitute the draft to send our sons to the Middle East to fight the terrorists. I cannot tell her what the right decision might be, as this is just something that everyone has to decide for themselves. All I can say is that I am so proud of the American sons and daughters who attend the service academies, as I spend a great deal of time with them at the U.S. Naval Academy.

With regard to dealing with a career choice and changing careers later in life, each person has to know himself or herself and decide for himself or herself what he or she wants out of life. While trying to survive the economic downturn, character issues, which are discussed later, enable one to cope in a more positive manner. It behooves us to look in other places for clues. One such place would be to note just how emerging markets survive financial turmoil, since that is a fact of life in these areas. Some financial experts view these unsettling times as an opportunity to implement new, aggressive, and bold ideas in order to increase their business and become more competitive with respect to their competition. These emerging businessmen see opportunities to increase customer loyalty and gain market share by altering the price structure of their products and refocusing their marketing.

As difficult as this concept may seem, as well as counterintuitive, when times are tough, encourage customers to trade up. By making the price increases much smaller, this signals to the consumer that they in fact are able to get premium products at a good value. Although this means a lower profit margin initially, such a tactic keeps the customer loyal to the brand. Keeping current customers is a lot easier than seeking new customers. Economic downturns or financial crisis events are great times to rethink just what the customers value. For example, from time to time I get phone calls from Verizon Wireless offering to give me a good deal on a new cellular phone if I sign a contract to use their service for two more years. A smarter approach would be to allow their customers to buy just as much service as they need, when they need it. Also they should allow the customers to buy minutes over their cell phone, on the Internet, at ATMs, or at kiosks in shopping malls. Many can make themselves more valuable to companies and employers by looking at new metrics such as macroeconomic measures, including inflation, unemployment, the exchange rate, and GDP per capita, and using this information to make new scenarios.

As individuals reinvent themselves by demonstrating adaptability, flexibility, and a good attitude, they should be aware that the more exceptional employees in a company, the better all of them will perform and the more likely it is that these outstanding employees will remain with the company. If these employees do not work well together, they will not benefit the company. Employees must seek to create a work culture that encourages cooperation and teamwork. The best security for individuals and companies is to stress the hiring, developing, motivating, and retraining of good people. Future employees seeking new jobs must have ideas and know the company so that he or she can be creative and suggest new ideas, new concepts.

One of the first questions I ask my students when I am a guest lecturer at the University of Maryland University College finance courses is about their present occupations. Most of them have some sort of government job, and they feel very secure, as they are trying to improve their lots in life by working on their MBA degrees. I stress to them that they should not feel so secure, as sometimes the external environment changes and their jobs may change or evaporate. I tell them that they are doing the right thing by preparing themselves with additional education, so that when change does occur they will be in a position to take advantage of any opportunities that arise. Change produces opportunity, and one just has to position himself to a better advantage.

I stress to them that now is the time to think of ways to differentiate themselves so that they will have a competitive advantage. Whoever their customers are in life will be the judge and jury of their advantage. Their perception is the only one that matters. Each person has to stand out because of his or her worth. Those who succeed will have to create overwhelming desirability. Besides creating competitive esteem, somehow each person has to demonstrate leadership and demonstrate that he can execute. Whether it is a company or a medical group, the leader and the group have to be involved in execution, as that is what it is all about. I caution my students that they have to know the people who work with them, and they have to set clear goals and priorities and then follow through. As I have said previously, they have to know themselves.

So it was with my decision to leave medicine in July 1995. I always planned to spend my entire career in medicine, but I did not know that the HMO system was coming, nor did I know just how bad the medical malpractice situation would be. Now it is very possible that the United States will have a socialized medical system like Europe.

Again, I can not tell anyone what sort of career changes to make, but I do tell eager students who are interested in going into medicine to go ahead and attend medical school. This will open up opportunities for them, and if they so choose, they do not have to practice medicine but can go into other fields with their MD degrees, such as finance, risk management, pharmaceutical research, genetic research, hospital administration, health care law, and the list goes on. And I give them the same advice that I give others about the military: know yourself and know how you see yourself fitting into this world. If one is not satisfied with his career or his station in life, one must have the strength and courage to make the necessary changes. One's attitude determines one's success. Career ideas do not just come out of the sky, so it is necessary to ask "what if" and to plan ahead.

Chapter Fourteen: International Medicine

International medicine can take numerous forms, as evidenced by the multitude of approaches used by the many participating institutions. Most examples of international medicine revolve around the improvement of medical knowledge and care by those in developed nations for those in emerging nations. The early examples of such expansion of knowledge can probably be traced to the medical missionaries who traveled to foreign countries to share medical knowledge as well as religious concepts. Since then many American and European medical schools and hospitals have helped health officials in other countries strengthen and improve their health systems at the regional and village levels.

Because of the high cost of medical and surgical care in the USA for those who do not have insurance, many Americans seek care abroad. At least eighty-five thousand Americans chose to travel each year for their needed medical procedures, according to a report by McKinsey & Company. According to the American Medical Association, surgical care can be obtained elsewhere for as little as 20 percent of the price of the same procedure in the USA.

Blue Cross Blue Shield of South Carolina has started a spin-off company, Companion Global Healthcare, which offers medical tourism services. Hannaford Supermarkets in Maine recently added an international option for hip replacements. Most of the patients going abroad are either uninsured or underinsured. Most of the medical tourism groups state that the quality of care elsewhere is often equal to or better than in the USA, as many countries have a high success rate, U.S.-trained doctors, and the most modern facilities.

However, Dr. Sharon Kleefield of Harvard Medical School says that there are no comprehensive data that adequately compare surgical services overseas with those delivered in the USA. The American Medical Association has issued guidelines on medical tourism at www.tinyurl.com/cpklcw. Additional information can be obtained by going to www.medicaltourismassociation.com and www. Jointcommissioninternational.org .

Recently the news in this field has concentrated on medical tourism and the breathtaking sums of money paid for a few Caribbean medical schools. Medical tourism has gained popularity in the USA because of the high cost of health care, particularly for those who are not insured. An example might be that of a person needing a coronary bypass operation, which could cost as much as $100,000 for someone without health insurance. The figure tossed about during the recent election was that there are about 45 million Americans without any health insurance. One alternative for these uninsured is to travel to another country for recommended surgical procedures. For instance, these persons could travel to South Korea, India, Latin America, or Mexico and have procedures done at much-reduced rates, even for $2,000. Now American medical centers see how medical tourism can be profitable, and they too are building medical facilities in other countries such as Panama. Both Johns Hopkins University and Harvard University are building hospitals in Panama City. An operation that costs $100,000 in the USA and $2,000 in India could cost $10,000 there.

The Caribbean medical schools have had the reputation of educating medical students from the USA who were not accepted to

American medical schools. There are about twenty-one such schools. But their reputations have improved because of several reasons. First, many of these schools now require that their graduates pass the USMLE (United States Medical Licensing Examination), the same required of American students. Secondly, many of these students spend their third and fourth years at various hospitals in the United States but usually not university teaching hospitals. As the U.S. population is growing and President Obama has promised to extend the government health programs to everyone, suddenly the health care planners realize that there are no provisions to increase the number of doctors in the United States. Additional doctors can be educated outside of the USA and can then immigrate to the USA. One Caribbean medical school was bought for $700 million, and another one was bought for $450 million. The number of applicants to all medical schools has increased exponentially, including these in the Caribbean.

Some medical centers in the USA are very committed to international medicine. Johns Hopkins International is the quintessential example of a dedicated medical school in this arena. They have established the Johns Hopkins International Medical Center in Singapore. This partnership will focus on the treatment and clinical research of solid tumors such as breast, colon, lung, and prostate. They will also concentrate on the treatment of liver, gastric, and nasopharyngeal cancers. In 2004 JHH opened a gynecologic surgery program. They will be expanding their liquid tumor research and treatment, such as for acute leukemia and bone marrow transplants. Already they have received Joint Commission accreditation. They promote rotations of health care professionals, lectures, observerships, and symposia, all of which facilitate knowledge transfer between Baltimore and Singapore.

The Clemenceau Medical Center in Beirut, Lebanon profited from JHH's participation from the very beginning. JHH worked with

Plaza Real Estate in planning this medical center. JHH reviewed the functional space and architectural plan for patient flow and services and provided human resources planning and management. They helped plan for the anticipated Joint Commission accreditation. They have managed the nursing organizational structure and will collaborate with the development of the clinical programs, the patient and quality management services, and educational packages for physicians, nurses, and the technical staff. They will also be doing joint research on several projects.

The MedCam Clinic is headquartered in Toronto, Canada, and works with Johns Hopkins Medical Center. There is a strategic consulting initiative on the clinical program development, and JHH provides guidance and assistance on the preparation for the Joint Commission accreditation. JHH also provides a medical second opinion for MedCam patients. A virtual reality program is used for clinics employing videoconferences, and there is a continuing medical education program for MedCam physicians. They are both exploring the opportunities for the development of ambulatory surgical clinics, advanced imaging centers, pain management clinics, and home health care solutions.

JHH also works with the Anadolu Medical Center in Turkey by providing consultation in architectural and engineering design. They have advised on the IT systems and on the capital equipment evaluation and purchases. JHH has consulted on the operating room efficiency, the radiology recruitment, and the Joint Commission compliance.

In Trinidad and Tobago, JHH has developed comprehensive medical programs that include screening, prevention, education, and the treatment of digestive disorders, cardiovascular diseases, diabetes, hearing loss, and language disorders. JHH has helped the health officials in Trinidad and Tobago develop biomedical research facilities.

As mentioned elsewhere, JHH has developed the Hospital Punta Pacific in Panama by providing some of the same services mentioned above. JHH will appoint a full-time Hopkins faculty member as medical director to monitor medical quality and patient safety as well as conduct educational events. JHH has also worked with Monterrey Tec and with Clinica Las Condes, providing some of the same services that have been provided to others.

The Jose De Mello Saude hospital group in Portugal collaborates with JHH in the areas of operating room management systems as well as other educational conferences.

Harvard University has also been working with many international medical centers. Examples include collaboration with the University of Queensland on the electronic medical records and research with Xinjiang Medical University in China.

The University of Pittsburgh will set up twenty-five oncology centers with GE Healthcare in the Middle East and Europe. George Washington has a relationship with many countries and their medical facilities. Much of their work consists of combating various diseases in a joint fashion.

Besides supporting a telemedicine system of providing a second opinion for patients in many countries, Israel has the Galil Telemedicine institute at the Technion University Medical Center in Haifa. Israel also trains physicians from many countries. They have developed the Applied Spectral Imaging Technology system, which gives pathologists from around the world second opinions on their diagnoses.

Telemedicine has additional applications. For example, an Australian group provides radiologists on a twenty-four-hour basis so American hospitals can utilize their services, particularly when the American radiologists are not available for coverage. A Baltimore group uses telemedicine to provide intensive care unit coverage for rural hospitals where there are no hospitalists to provide care on a twenty-four-hour basis.

Now comes the best part of this topic, as I am organizing with Dr. Ben Sachs, the Dean of the Tulane University Medical School, Tulane International. Although Tulane University already has some facility or activity on every continent in the world, we are preparing to work with various medical schools to improve their curricula and the quality of their graduates. The activity that already exists consists of research and treatment of various diseases such as HIV/AIDs and various infectious diseases in the tropics. I look forward to this new assignment.

Chapter Fifteen:
Life Worthwhile

Throughout my life I have participated in various extracurricular activities. When I first started practicing neurosurgery, I could not be far from the telephone. So learning to play tennis was the easiest outlet for me at that time. I went to the Annapolis Racquet Club and took lessons from Dennis Quigley. This sport allowed me to play on a regular basis with several of the other doctors and was an outlet when we went on vacations, especially to the Caribbean and to Hawaii.

As the years went by, I became more interested in yacht racing, so I learned to sail at the Annapolis Sailing Center. My first sailboat was a Tartan 27 and was called the *L5-S1*, after the bones in the back that I operated on frequently. I raced with the Annapolis Yacht Club and the Chesapeake Bay Yacht Racing Association for twenty-five years. Other boats I had were a Pearson 30 named *The Beagle*, a C&C 34R named *Forever Fifty*, and a J105 named *Suddenly Sixty*. *The Beagle* was so named because around the time I bought it, I took the family to Machu Picchu in Peru and went to areas Darwin had visited years ago. *Forever Fifty* and *Suddenly Sixty* were named by Judith Viorst, who wrote poems and small books with those names.

As the years went by, I became more interested in golfing and joined the U.S. Naval Academy Golf Association nearby. I have been playing golf since 1990 and have a high handicap. The guys at the Navy Golf

Association are great and a lot of fun. Although the origin of the U.S. Naval Academy Golf Course is somewhat murky, the earliest records indicate that in 1916 the first golf course was a nine-hole course built at what now is Perry Circle. But there is evidence in an article in *The New York Times* that there was a golf course available to personnel at the U.S. Naval Academy November 18, 1895, located on a government farm.

Through the years numerous admirals and generals have played golf at this course. In 1941 Gene Sarazen and Sam Snead played an exhibition match against Admiral Wilson and Captain Pollard. On May 18, 1953, President Dwight D. Eisenhower enjoyed eighteen holes of golf with Admiral C. Turner Joy. Presently the golf team at the U.S. Naval Academy plays their home matches on the course, and twice a year the Academy hosts the Patriot League invitational tournaments.

I have always wondered just who all the admirals and generals were who played this course. The present chairman of the Joint Chiefs of Staff, Admiral Mike Mullen, played there frequently until he assumed the responsibilities of his present job. The golf pro is Mr. Pat Owen, the coach of the Navy golf team and the head pro at the club. One of the most valuable assets of the U.S. Naval Academy Golf Association is Mr. Bill Matton. Bill arranges for all of the tournaments and keeps everyone in the club busy throughout the entire golfing season. He arranges and schedules a medal play each month, a scramble in the spring and in the fall, a championship for the seniors, a Gold Tee Knockout, a Commandant's Cup, a club championship, a grandparent-parent child championship, and a President's Cup. But the seminal and archetypal event each year is the member-guest tournament in June. This is an opportunity for members to bring the best player they know to the course or to bring an acquaintance to Annapolis just to have a good time. I have participated in this event numerous times and have brought Dr. Dick Cooper, Mr. Rick Gibb, and Mr. Jim Handlon as my guest partners.

After a trip to Argentina I became interested in learning the Argentine Tango. I started taking lessons at Arthur Murray Dancing Studio. My teacher and partner was Daria Zotova from Russia. She not only taught me the Argentine Tango, but she taught me about twenty-five other dances, which enabled us to win first place at the Harrisburg Showcase in March 2007, first place at the World Dance-o-Rama at Las Vegas at the MGM Grand Hotel in May 2007 and again at the Harrisburg Showcase in March 2008 at a higher level. These dances included the Foxtrot, American tango, Hustle, swing, West Coast swing, waltz, Viennese waltz, quickstep, Peabody, rumba, cha-cha, samba, salsa, merengue, polka, country waltz, country two-step, country cha-cha, and country swing. All of these were done in the open and closed competition. Because of a knee injury, I have put dancing on hold.

Chapter Sixteen:
Surviving the Economic Downturn

The world economy is moving rapidly and inexorably toward a deteriorating situation, and soon everyone will have to take some sort of action. It may become necessary for you to get a second job and cut your expenses immediately. In an economic downturn, entrepreneurship typically increases. New companies are started that improve the lives of everyone. You may have to reinvent yourself. You will not survive if you wallow, flounder, welter, and deny reality. If you have the entrepreneurial spirit, you might want to access http://www.thevirtualhandshake.com for additional information about securing funding and making connections.

In order to reinvent yourself or to survive, you have to think about creating such a competitive advantage that you will be overwhelmingly desirable to any employer or customer. They will be the judge and jury of your efforts. The perception of those who might hire you is the only reality that matters. You want to stand out because of your value. You can't be just another gray box, but a clear and obvious choice with a clear value. Victory goes to those who focus their efforts to create overwhelming odds at the point of contact. Then it will be necessary to demonstrate that you are a leader.

Execution is the major job of a business leader. Execution is a discipline and an integral part of any strategy. If you are seeking any job in business, know your people and your business. Insist on realism. Set clear goals and priorities. Your attitude makes all the difference in the world. Follow through. Know yourself. If you find that you need to change the behavior of your fellow workers, remember that the foundation of changing behavior is linking rewards to performance and making the linkages transparent.

In addition to reinventing oneself, it is mandatory to take an inventory of the net assets in one's portfolio. Owning property does not give one security, but it may give your creditors security. Driving around Detroit, Memphis, California, or Florida demonstrates that property in itself is not the security people can rely on. Foreclosure signs and for-sale signs can be seen in all of these locations and in other places. Many people bought into the below-prime mortgages and hoped that the price of real estate would continue its upward spiral, only to learn that the value of real estate can also plummet. Unless it is too late, the best position is to not have any debt, including a mortgage on your house.

Many people have been relying on the government to provide them with a certain amount of security. Even though the United States has something of a welfare system, we all learned after Hurricane Katrina that government programs do not work all the time. Despite some of the best-intentioned efforts of Congress, some factors negate some plans, such as the graying of the American population and the high cost of private health care.

As I write this, President Obama's administration is planning an expansion of government health care piecemeal, i.e., increasing government involvement in covering children, the unemployed, and poor people, and reducing the age of Medicare eligibility from sixty-five to fifty. In addition, plans are being considered to change the method of reimbursement for physicians to a bundle payment for a particular problem, such as paying one price for a total hip replacement or one price for treating a certain type of cancer. In order to survive this economic downturn, it will be necessary to be very vigilant of the various health care proposals and to measure your coverage with any alternatives.

Although a steady, reliable income is perhaps one of the best methods of survival, that is not always the situation people find themselves in during an economic downturn. One way to survive such a situation is to plan ahead and invest in a company whose management you know and whose products are needed. Another business variation with which I have been involved is the creation of a business that makes good corporations great and great corporations outstanding. While working with Mr. Jim Handlon, we strove to partner with companies in order to drive results. We identified growth opportunities and implemented goals. We focused on top line acceleration and bottom-line results by providing high-horsepower talent and executives. We were accountable for delivering results and would share in the success. Our company would take equity as part of the arrangement, and we would create a winning strategy and lead in its implementation. In addition to working with established companies, we also worked with international startups.

I was impressed by an action one company is taking in order to be more competitive. Hyundai, a Korean car manufacturer, is now advertising that if a customer buys a car from them on the installment plan and sometime during the following year loses his or her job, Hyundai will take the new car back at no additional cost to the customer. That is an innovative policy, which will go a long way toward survival.

I will now refer you to a Web site and a book. Ben Sherwood calls the book *The Survivors Club,* and the site is http://www.thesurvivorsclub. org. You will find a series of questions to help classify you and your reaction to your situation. He has studied all sorts of survivors and describes many different survivors in his book. He has tried to see what common thread runs through the various survivors and has classified them into several groups, such as those who are thinkers, those who are fighters, those who are realistic, those who are connectors, and those who are believers.

I think he would classify Liam Neeson in the movie *Taken* as a fighter, as he survived unbelievable odds. In addition, another example of a fighter and survivor has to be Ben Roethlisberger, quarterback for the Pittsburgh Steelers. Often during the Super Bowl when he seemed to be surrounded and in trouble with members of the St. Louis Cardinals defense, somehow he liberated himself and threw a long pass to a receiver down field; he would save the play and make significant gains. As we try to survive, we need to exert competitive behavior and remain committed to surviving with mental fitness.

CHAPTER SEVENTEEN:
REUNION

Sometimes, but not frequently, we have an opportunity to revisit our past, to refresh our memories about various events, and to discover what happened to all those people with whom we shared our youth. Several months ago I thought about our neighborhood in Montgomery, Alabama, and wondered what happened to our playmates. I then tracked down sixteen former neighbors with whom I shared National Street and arranged for a reunion, which occurred February 27, 2009. We all gathered for a dinner at a resort in Birmingham.

It was such a pleasure to see all of these people and to listen to them talk about their lives. Although many were not always so certain that our parents had known what they were doing, our parents must have known something, as the neighborhood produced four doctors, four lawyers, two engineers, one professional football player, one schoolteacher, one dance teacher, and a few business and insurance people. Two of the doctors became professors of medicine, one at Yale and one at the University of Michigan. One of the lawyers became a judge in Montgomery. Each person was given the opportunity to speak at the reunion, to relate where he or she lived, what he or she did, and any other information they wanted to share.

My brother Sheldon related an experience he had when he was an obstetrical resident at the University of Cincinnati. At that time most of the patients were poor and black, and some were in the Black Panther movement. They knew that Sheldon had a Southern accent and made life uncomfortable for him. Sheldon became discouraged and decided to visit Bart Starr in Green Bay, Wisconsin. Bart admonished him not to allow ignorant people filled with hatred to derail his career aspirations.

Later in life Sheldon had an opportunity to counsel an aspiring doctor who was unfortunate enough to have been born with hydrocephalus. As a result, this doctor had many ventriculo-atrial shunts to divert the cerebrospinal fluid, but surprisingly he survived and thrived and had above-average intelligence, which is unusual for someone with this problem. The patient told Sheldon that because of his enlarged head, he did not think he could make it through a pediatric residency. Sheldon gave him the same advice Bart gave him years ago and counseled him not to let ignorant people filled with hatred and prejudice wreck his career. That patient now is treating patients in Africa who have AIDS.

Another interesting speaker was Bart Starr, former quarterback for the Green Bay Packers. Bart talked about interesting people one meets throughout life, some of whom have an influence. He then recited a favorite quote of his: "Some people come into our lives and quickly go, like waves briefly touching the shore. Some people stay for a while and give us a deeper understanding of what is truly important in this life. They touch our souls. We gain strength from the footprints they have left on our hearts, and we will never, ever be the same." The evening reminded Bart of this quote as he listened to the others give details of their lives. Bart spoke about the influence Vince Lombardi had on his life and upon the lives of others.

That same weekend I attended the forty-fifth reunion of my medical school class from the University of Alabama. Back in 1960 we started out with eighty classmates, and four years later sixty of us graduated. Fifteen classmates have passed away, and approximately twenty-five members attended the event. The various members represented almost all of the medical specialties and practiced medicine in many areas of the country. Now some have retired and others are considering retirement, but they are concerned about the economic downturn and think they cannot afford retirement. Dr. Alan Siegal related his relationship with Dr. Tinsley Harrison, who was one of the icons of medicine and taught most of us at various times. Others talked about some of their experiences and families.

Both of these reunions enabled us to talk about surviving the future during these unusual times. After reuniting with many of my friends at these various reunions, Annetta and I are spending more time with our grandchildren. We took Larry and Reyna and their children, Alison and Harrison, to the Galapagos this past Christmas. The children really enjoyed the trip and are anxious to have more unusual journeys. Reyna is the Chairperson of the Department of Science at the Madeira School in McLean, Virginia. She teaches several courses of A.P. Physics. Larry is chairman of the Department of History and Government at the same school. Larry graduated from Harvard when Reyna graduated from Wellesley, and they met teaching at a boarding school near Sheffield, Massachusetts.

I am spending more time working with the Dean of the Tulane Medical School, trying to expand Tulane into South America. We are looking for several medical schools with which to partner. In addition, I will be giving a speech on surviving the economic crisis live via Internet to a conference in Croatia associated with the University of Zagreb on May 22, 2009, and will be giving a talk on international medicine to the World Forum in Washington DC on July 2, 2009. I wrote this book because we, the Hall of Fame inductees, were encouraged to write such a book after being inducted into the Hall of Fame at Oxford University in August 2008 and to tie our lives into what we are doing today.

BIBLIOGRAPHY

1. Alexander, Eben, Jr., "Courtland Harwell Davis, Jr." *Surgical Neurology* 27 (1987):105–106.

2. Berg, Julie Dexter, John M. Matthews, and Constance M. O'Hare. "Measuring Brand Health to Improve Top-Line Growth." *Wall Street Journal*, March 23, 2009.

3. Berthon, Pierre, Morris B. Holbrook, and James M. Hulbert. "Understanding and Managing the Brand Space." *Wall Street Journal*, March 23, 2009.

4. Bossidy, Larry and Ram Charan, *Execution: The Discipline of Getting Things Done* (New York: Crown Business, 2002), 20–31, 57–72.

5. Brinkley, Douglas, *The Great Deluge* (New York: William Morrow, 2006), 716, 323–330.

6. Brooks, Geraldine, *A Year of Wonders: A Novel of the Plague* (New York: Viking Press, 2001), 308, 1–100

7. Chakravarthy, Bala. "A New Strategy Framework for Coping With Turbulence." *Wall Street Journal*, March 23, 2009.

8. Crosby, Elizabeth C., Tryphena Humphrey, and Edward W. Lauer, *Correlative Anatomy of the Nervous System*, (New York: The Macmillan Company, 1962), 731.

9. Day, George S. and David J. Reibstein, *Wharton on Dynamic Competitive Strategy* (New York: John Wiley and Sons, Inc., 1997), 20–75.

10. Dyer, John P., *Tulane: The Biography of a University, 1834–1965* (New York: Harper & Row, 1966), 370, 1–200.

11. Fall, Bernard B., *Street Without Joy: Indochina at War 1946–1954* (Harrisburg, PA: The Stackpole Company, 1961), 322.

12. Fall, Bernard B., *Viet-Nam Witness, 1953–66* (New York: Frederick A. Praeger, 1966), 363.

13. Fall, Bernard B., *The Two Vietnams: A Political and Military Analysis* (New York: Frederick A. Praeger, 1963), 498.

14. Ferguson, Niall, *The Ascent of Money* (New York: The Penguin Press, 2008), 219, 278.

15. Horwitz, Norman and Hugo V. Rizzoli, *Postoperative Complications of Intracranial Neurological Surgery* (Baltimore: Williams & Wilkins, 1982), 472.

16. Karnow, Stanley, *Vietnam: A History: The First Complete Account of Vietnam at War* (New York: The Viking Press, 1983), 752, 387–426.

17. Kushner, Jack, *Preparing to Tack: When Physicians Change Careers* (New York: Vantage Press, Inc., 1995), 14–20.

18. Loewen, James W., *Lies My Teacher Told Me* (New York: Simon & Schuster, 1995), 246–247.

19. Mathers, Helen, *Steel City Scholars: The Centenary History of the University of Sheffield* (London: James & James, 2005), 466, 100–250.

20. Mohr, Clarence L. and Joseph E. Gordon, *Tulane: The Emergence of a Modern University, 1945–1980* (Baton Rouge, LA: Louisiana State University Press, 2001), 540, 175–300.

21. Sanua, Marianne R., *Here's To Our Fraternity: One Hundred Years of Zeta Beta   Tau, 1898–1998.* (Hanover and London: Zeta Beta Tau Foundation/Brandeis, 1998), 319, 150–275.

22. Sherwood, Ben, *The Survivors Club: The Secrets and Science That Could Save Your Life* (New York: Grand Central Publishing, 2009), 306–312, 311–326.

23. Treacy, Michael and Fred Wiersema, *The Discipline of Market Leaders* (New York: Perseus Books, 1995), 17–26.

24. Tulane University, *Tulane University: Renaissance* (Nashville, TN: The Booksmith Group, 2007), 115, 25–90.

25. Viorst, Judith, *Necessary Losses* (New York: Simon & Schuster, 1986), 447, 205–222.

26. Viorst, Judith, *Forever Fifty and Other Negotiations* (New York: Thorndike Press, 1990).

27. Viorst, Judith, *Suddenly Sixty* (New York: Simon & Schuster, 2000), 79.

Web Sites

http://www.thesurvivorsclub.org

http://www.bio-guard.net

http://www.thevirtualhandshake.com

http://www.jhint.net/glo/projects/

http://www.gwumc.edu/imp/downloads/International_activities_database.pdf

http://www.google.com/search?hl=en+q=university+of+Pittsburgh+oncology+clinics

http://qatar-weill.cornell.edu/

http://www.sloanreview.mit.edu/wsj

NOTES

1 - Lingerie on the Fountain

Although I did not quote any lines in F. Scott Fitzgerald's book, *The Great Gatsby*, one can get a glimpse of the Fitzgerald lifestyle by reading this book (initially published April 10, 1925, by Charles Scribner's Sons in New York). The information about their parties was drawn from conversations with numerous citizens of Montgomery, Alabama, who remembered those years.

3 - Not as a Stranger

State Fair is a play that was selected by the drama teacher at Sidney Lanier High School. The play was dramatized by Luella McMahon and Christopher Sergel from the book by Phil Stong and published in 1953 by The Dramatic Company.

4 - Years of Wonder

Most of the information used in this chapter was from my personal memory. Several books that I have read and enjoyed, such as *Here's To Our Fraternity: One Hundred Years of Zeta Beta Tau,* may have influenced me. Additional books that influenced my thinking include *Tulane: The Biography of a University, Tulane: The Emergence of a Modern University, Steel City Scholars: The Centenary History of the University of Sheffield,* and *Year of Wonder* by Geraldine Brooks

6 - Street Without Joy

My association with Bernard Fall and reading his three books cited in the bibliography influenced some of my thoughts on the Vietnam War. The photos that went around the world are in *Lies My Teacher Told Me* by James Loewen. Dr. Edgar Kahn and Dr. Elizabeth Crosby wrote their respective books, which are cited in the bibliography.

7 – Only Surgeons Win In War

The book about the history of Vietnam by Stanley Karnow added to the information I gathered by serving in Vietnam.

8 – Neurosurgical Giants

In this chapter I used some of the material I had previously published about Dr. Eben Alexander in *Preparing to Tack: When Physicians Change Careers* in Chapter 3. I used notes about Dr. Courtland Davis and Dr. David Kelly, which each of them sent to me for inclusion in this book.

9 - Neurosurgery Where George Washington Resigned His Commission

Material for this chapter was derived in part from a letter written to me by Mr. Skip Conover.

10 - Tacking: Changing Careers

Mr. Jim Hanlon furnished information to me about Bottom-Line Partners.

12 - Green Wave and Midshipmen

Although I am very familiar with what has happened at Tulane University, *The Great Deluge* by Douglas Brinkley may have influenced me. I also read *Tulane Renaissance*. Some of my material was derived from speeches and presentations given by President Scott Cowen and from written information from Tulane in various publications.

14 - International Medicine

A great deal of the information in this chapter was derived from personal experience working in this space. I also researched several Web sites, which are noted above.

15 - Life Worthwhile

The information concerning the origins of the U.S. Naval Academy Golf Course was obtained from old notes and essays provided to me by Mr. Pat Owen, the Golf Pro and Coach of the Navy Golf team. This material was never published.

16 - Surviving the Economic Downturn

I have read *The Ascent of Money* by Niall Ferguson, and some of his ideas may have found their way into this book. Also, Ben Sherwood has written a delightful book, *The Survivors Club,* and I enjoyed taking the test on the Web site. I have also read the books written by Larry Bossidy and Ram Charan, George Day and David Reibstein, and Michael Treacy and Fred Wiersema, all of which are excellent and are listed in the bibliography. I have also visited the Virtual Handshake Web site.